Questions & Answers:

# Employment Discrimination

## Carolina Academic Press
## Questions & Answers Series

**Questions & Answers: Administrative Law, Fourth Edition**
Linda D. Jellum, Karen A. Jordan

**Questions & Answers: Antitrust**
Shubha Ghosh

**Questions & Answers: Bankruptcy, Second Edition**
Mary Jo Wiggins

**Questions & Answers: Business Associations, Second Edition**
Douglas M. Branson

**Questions & Answers: Civil Procedure, Fifth Edition**
William V. Dorsaneo, III, Elizabeth Thornburg, Brooke D. Coleman

**Questions & Answers: Constitutional Law, Third Edition**
Paul E. McGreal, Linda S. Eads, Charles W. Rhodes

**Questions & Answers: Contracts, Third Edition**
Scott J. Burnham

**Questions & Answers: Copyright Law, Second Edition**
Dave Fagundes, Robert C. Lind

**Questions & Answers: Criminal Law, Fifth Edition**
Paul Marcus

**Questions & Answers: Criminal Procedure — Police Investigation, Fourth Edition**
Wayne A. Logan

**Questions & Answers: Criminal Procedure — Prosecution and Adjudication, Fourth Edition**
Wayne A. Logan

**Questions & Answers: Employment Discrimination**
Marcia L. McCormick

**Questions & Answers: Environmental Law**
Dru Stevenson

**Questions & Answers: Evidence, Fourth Edition**
Paul C. Giannelli

**Questions & Answers: Family Law, Fourth Edition**
Mark Strasser

**Questions & Answers: Federal Estate & Gift, Taxation, Third Edition**
James M. Delaney, Elaine Hightower Gagliardi

**Questions & Answers: Federal Income Tax, Second Edition**
James M. Delaney

**Questions & Answers: Intellectual Property, Third Edition**
Gary Myers, Lee Ann Wheelis Lockridge

**Questions & Answers: International Law**
Rebecca Bratspies

**Questions & Answers: Patent Law**
Cynthia M. Ho

**Questions & Answers: Payment Systems, Second Edition**
Timothy R. Zinnecker

**Questions & Answers: Professional Responsibility, Fifth Edition**
Patrick Emery Longan

**Questions & Answers: Property, Third Edition**
John Copeland Nagle, Donald J. Kochan

**Questions & Answers: Remedies, Second Edition**
Rachel M. Janutis, Thomas O. Main

**Questions & Answers: Secured Transactions, Fourth Edition**
Bruce A. Markell, Timothy R. Zinnecker

**Questions & Answers: The First Amendment, Fourth Edition**
Russell L. Weaver, William D. Araiza

**Questions & Answers: Torts, Fifth Edition**
Anita Bernstein

**Questions & Answers: Trademark and Unfair Competition**
Vince F. Chiappetta

**Questions & Answers: Wills, Trusts, and Estates, Third Edition**
Thomas M. Featherston, Jr.

# Questions & Answers: Employment Discrimination

*Multiple Choice and Short Answer Questions and Answers*


**Marcia L. McCormick**

Professor and Co-Director
William C. Wefel Center for Employment Law
Saint Louis University School of Law



Carolina Academic Press
Durham, North Carolina

ISBN: 978-1-5310-2391-1
eISBN: 978-1-5310-2392-8
LCCN: 2022948444

Carolina Academic Press
700 Kent Street
Durham, NC 27701
(919) 489-7486
www.cap-press.com

Printed in the United States of America

# Table of Contents

# Preface

This study guide is written as a survey of most topics covered in Employment Discrimination Law courses in law schools. Although the structure of some casebooks or particular courses may vary from the structure of this volume, it tracks the structure that I have found most useful for teaching: starting with basic coverage questions and remedies, moving to the main frameworks for analyzing discrimination, and then spending more concentrated time on specific issues related to classes protected by Title VII, the Age Discrimination in Employment Act, and the Americans with Disabilities Act.

Employment discrimination law in the courts is not always settled. There are number of controversies and circuit splits on relevant issues. Moreover, a number of issues worth exploring relate to policy or large questions about the definitions of discrimination and protected classes. As a result, this volume has more open-ended questions and more policy-type questions than at least some other volumes in the Q & A series. These kinds of questions do not have "right" answers in the usual sense, and so the answers provided are just one option of a response. Some answers explicitly note this and simply give guidance about the kinds of things students might explore. Similar caveats apply to the answers to the exam questions, additional issue spotter, and additional short essay questions at the end of the volume.

Lastly, the practice of employment discrimination law is often viewed as highly technical, with specialized frameworks for analyzing different kinds of adverse employment actions and discriminatory environments. Because the Supreme Court has generally *not* engaged in those efforts towards complexity, and in fact has pushed back repeatedly to keep the legal question fairly straightforward, this volume does not engage with some of those more detailed frameworks, like for reductions in force, discriminatory discipline, etc. The explanations hint at some of this complexity, but the questions do not tackle it head-on. I welcome any and all feedback from readers including additional areas to cover in future editions.

Marcia L. McCormick
St. Louis, Missouri
marcia.mccormick@slu.edu

# About the Author

**Marcia L. McCormick** is a Professor and Co-Director of the William C. Wefel Center for Employment Law at St. Louis University School of Law. McCormick began her legal career as a staff attorney with the International Human Rights Law Institute, where she directed analysis and research of allegations of sexual violence committed during the war in what was formerly known as Yugoslavia. She then went to the Illinois Attorney General's Office where she litigated civil appeals in state and federal courts. She left the Illinois Attorney General's Office to join the faculty at Chicago-Kent College of Law at the Illinois Institute of Technology. McCormick then moved on to Cumberland Law School at Samford University, before coming to SLU LAW. Professor McCormick's work has been published in a variety of law journals, including the *Berkeley Journal of Labor & Employment Law*, the *University of Pennsylvania Journal of Constitutional Law*, the *Indiana Law Review*, and others. She has contributed to several books, and co-authors a leading casebook on Employment Discrimination Law and a leading treatise and hornbook on Employment Law. She is also frequently sought out by the media for legal analysis of civil rights issues.

# Questions

Topic 1 Questions

# General Overview of Applicable Law, Enforcement, and Remedies

1.1 How many commissioners serve on the Equal Employment Opportunity Commission?

1.2 How did Congress attempt to avoid the Commission being biased?

A. A certain number of members have to come from the labor side and a certain number from management.

B. A certain number of members have to come from a political party different from the others.

C. The members are appointed with life tenure and salary protections under Article III of the Constitution.

D. The members serve at the will of Congress.

1.3 Alabama has no state fair employment practices agency. How many days from the adverse employment action does an aggrieved person have to file a charge with the Equal Employment Opportunity Commission?

A. 30 days

B. 90 days

C. 180 days

D. 300 days

**1.4** Illinois, like 46 other states and the District of Columbia, has a statute that prohibits employment discrimination on the same bases (and additional ones) as Title VII. It also has agencies that enforce that statute. How many days from the adverse employment action does an aggrieved person in Illinois have to file a charge with the Equal Employment Opportunity Commission?

A. 30 days

B. 90 days

C. 180 days

D. 300 days

**1.5** If an aggrieved person files with the appropriate state agency first, when can the EEOC begin its proceedings, assuming a worksharing agreement?

A. Immediately

B. 10 days later

C. 30 days later

D. 60 days later

**1.6** If the Commission finds no cause to believe that discrimination has occurred, what effect does that have on a person's charge and later proceedings?

A. The person's charge is dismissed, and the matter is closed.

B. The person's charge is dismissed, and the person can bring an action in state or federal court after requesting and receiving a right to sue letter.

C. The person can seek judicial review of the Commission's decision in federal court, and the federal court reviews the decision for substantial evidence.

D. The person's charge is dismissed, and the matter is res judicata in the federal system, but the person can still proceed in state court.

**1.7** How many days after receiving a right to sue letter does a person have to file an action in court?

A. 30 days

B. 60 days

C. 90 days

D. 180 days

**1.8** How long does the Commission have to investigate a charge and make a determination as to cause?

A. 30 days

B. 60 days

C. 120 days

D. There is no absolute limit, but if the Commission hasn't finished the investigation within 180 days, a person can ask for a right to sue letter.

**1.9** Which of the following practices does Title VII expressly prohibit? Select all that apply.

A. Deciding not to hire an African American person because of that person's race.

B. Requiring all applicants to pass an intelligence test for an entry-level sales job, where the test excludes more members of one race than another, without proof that the test is job related and consistent with business necessity.

C. Asking an applicant when she is likely to have children.

D. Asking an applicant what religion he or she is.

E. Publishing an advertisement seeking only women when being female is not a bona fide occupational qualification.

**1.10** Who is prohibited from discriminating under Title VII against whom? Select all that apply.

A. Educational institutions for discrimination against students

B. Private clubs for discrimination in membership decisions

C. A business with 20 employees for discrimination against those employees

D. A business with 9 employees for discrimination against those employees

E. A business for discrimination against customers

F. Labor unions for discrimination against those they represent

G. Employment agencies for discrimination against people who want to use them to get jobs

H. A hospital for discriminating against patients

**1.11** Under the ADEA, who is prohibited from discriminating against whom? Select all that apply.

A. Educational institutions for discrimination against old students.

B. Private clubs for discrimination in membership decisions.

C. A business with 20 employees for discrimination against employees who are 40 and older because of age.

D. A business with 20 employees for discrimination against employees under 40 because of age.

E. A business with 17 employees for discrimination against employees 40 and older.

F. A business for discrimination against customers.

G. Employment agencies for discrimination against people who want to use them to get jobs.

H. A hospital for discriminating against patients.

**1.12** Which of the following entities are covered by Title I of the ADA? (select all that apply)

A. An educational institution discriminating against a student.

B. An employment agency discriminating against people who apply to be placed with an employer.

C. An employer who has 10 employees discriminating against one of them.

D. An employer with 20 employees discriminating against one of them.

E. A labor organization discriminating against one of its members.

F. A private country club discriminating against one of its members.

**1.13** Arden worked for Store, Co. for five years, when they were assigned a new supervisor. That supervisor began harassing Arden for using they/them pronouns, insisting that Arden use the gendered pronouns that matched the sex on Arden's birth certificate. Arden notified their manager about the harassment, but the manager told Arden to "toughen up." Arden started being assigned only the worst shifts, and when they complained, Arden was told, "snitches get stitches. Be glad this is the only fallout." One day, Arden's supervisor told them they would have to work that Sunday. Arden said they could not because they had a church obligation and offered to find a co-worker to take the shift. Arden's supervisor said that if Arden didn't come to work that Sunday, they would be fired. Arden went to church instead and was fired.

Arden filed a charge with the EEOC, marking on the charge form that they had experienced sex-based harassment and retaliation. After the EEOC issued a right to sue letter, Arden filed a lawsuit in an appropriate court, claiming injuries from sex-based harassment, retaliation, and religious discrimination for failing to accommodate Arden's need to go to church the day they were fired. Store Co. won a trial on the harassment and retaliation claims but lost on the religious discrimination claim. On appeal, Store Co. argued for the first time that the trial court lacked jurisdiction over the religion claim because Arden had failed to exhaust administrative remedies for it. How is the Court of Appeals likely to rule?

A. In favor of Store, Co., because without an EEOC investigation on the religion claim, Store Co.'s due process rights were violated.

B. In favor of Store, Co., because Arden's charge did not include the religion claim.

C. In favor of Arden, because filing a charge is not a jurisdictional prerequisite and Store Co. waived its exhaustion argument by fully litigating the religion claim.

D. In favor of Arden under the harmless error doctrine, since the trial court clearly had jurisdiction over the other two claims.

**1.14** Chris is a receptionist at a clinic that has ten support staff (including Chris), and six doctors, who are partners in the medical practice. The personnel manager fires Chris because of sex. Can Chris bring a claim against the clinic under Title VII?

A. Yes, because the clinic has enough employees to meet Title VII's coverage requirement.

B. Yes, because Chris is clearly an employee of the clinic.

C. No, unless the structure of the partnership provides that the doctors are subject to enough control by clinic administrators to make them employees.

D. No, because there are not enough employees to satisfy Title VII's coverage requirements.

**1.15** If Chris were fired for being 40 years old, would the answer be different?

**1.16** If Chris were fired because of a disability, would the answer be different?

**1.17** Blair is a student at State University, who is earning course credit for an internship. If Blair's internship supervisor harasses Blair on the basis of race, can Blair bring a Title VII action?

A. No, because interns are never protected by Title VII.

B. No, as long as the internship is unpaid and is supervised by the University in some way.

C. Yes, because harassment is just another form of discrimination.

D. Yes, because Blair is being deprived of equal educational opportunities.

**1.18** Alex is an associate at a law firm. When the time comes to apply for partner, Alex applies, but is not promoted. The reason given was that Alex was too feminine to be a good partner. Can Alex bring a Title VII claim?

A. Yes, because promotions are terms, conditions, and privileges of employment.

B. Yes, because denial of a promotion is explicitly listed as an adverse employment action under Title VII.

C. No, because partners aren't employees, and so not protected by Title VII.

D. No, because law firms are partnerships, and so not covered by Title VII.

**1.19** In *Patterson v. McLean Credit Union*, 491 U.S. 164 (1989), and *McDonald v. Santa Fe Trail Transportation Co.*, 427 U.S. 273 (1976), the Supreme court recognized that race-based employment discrimination would violate a statute other than Title VII: 42 U.S.C. § 1981. Why does that statute apply?

A. Because every employment relationship is a contract.

B. Because the plaintiffs in those cases had written employment contracts.

C. Because § 1981 by its terms prohibits certain employment practices.

D. Because race discrimination in employment is a "badge or incident" of slavery.

**1.20** What are the Commission's powers under Title VII? Select all that apply.

A. Investigate charges.

B. Conciliate disputes.

C. Bring a civil action in federal court against an employer believed to have violated the act.

D. Adjudicate claims of discrimination.

E. Impose civil fines against employers found to have violated the act.

F. Issue cease and desist orders against employers found to have violated the act.

G. Petition the Attorney General to institute criminal proceedings.

**1.21** What relief can a successful plaintiff get in a disparate impact suit?

A. Compensatory damages

B. Punitive damages

C. Reinstatement

D. Back pay

E. Injunctive relief other than reinstatement or back pay

F. Attorneys fees and costs

**1.22** What relief can a successful disparate treatment plaintiff be awarded?

A. Compensatory damages

B. Punitive damages

C. Reinstatement

D. Back pay

E. Injunctive relief other than reinstatement and back pay

F. Attorneys fees and costs

**1.23** How do the Commission's rulemaking powers differ between Title VII and Title I of the ADA?

**1.24** True or false: If an employer is found by a court to have engaged in race discrimination against African Americans in promotions and agrees in a settlement to save a certain part of promotions for a short period of time for qualified members of that group, Caucasian employees can later sue the employer for disparate treatment for complying with that agreement.

**1.25** Jo's employer has a comprehensive antiharassment policy with clear instructions for reporting, and opportunities to report to several different people, bypassing an employee's own supervisor. Jo's supervisor repeatedly offered her money for sex, called her mobile phone and left sexually suggestive messages, and threatened to kidnap her and take her to another state. Jo did not report the harassment or otherwise take advantage of the antiharassment policy. She rebuffed the advances, though, and then she was fired. If, after exhausting her administrative remedies, Jo sues her supervisor under Title VII, what is the most likely result?

A. A win for Jo. This is straightforward quid pro quo harassment that results in automatic liability.

B. A win for Jo. Title VII defines employer to include agents of the employer, and supervisors who take tangible employment actions are agents of the employer.

C. A loss for Jo. Courts have generally found that individuals who discriminate are not liable under Title VII.

D. A loss for Jo. Jo didn't follow the employer's antiharassment policy and so may not now bring a claim.

# Analytical Frameworks: Disparate Treatment and Disparate Impact Basics

2.1 What is the main difference between disparate treatment and disparate impact?

2.2 Golden City and its surrounding suburbs are like many larger and mid-size cities in the U.S. in that neighborhoods are racially segregated. The majority of the City's population is Black (75%), 15% is Latino, and 10% is white or another race. In the suburbs, the population is predominantly white: 80% are white, 12% are Asian, 6% are Black, and the remaining 2% are Latino or another race. Edgar James, Inc., a regional brokerage company, has offices throughout the region. The company hires employees of all races, but it assigns white employees almost exclusively to suburban offices, and Black employees almost exclusively to offices in the City on the logic that having Black brokers will attract more business from Black customers. Because salary depends on sales, and sales tend to be higher in the suburbs, those assigned to suburban offices tend to make more than those in the City.

John Williams is a Black broker assigned to an office in the city. If he sues Edgar James for race discrimination, is he likely to be successful?

A. Yes, because the employer is using race to assign employees to particular locations.

B. Yes, because the segregation in the region creates a disparate impact on Black employees.

C. No, because attracting customers is a Bona Fide Occupational Qualification for this position.

D. No, because the company is trying to expand financial opportunities to underserved populations, which makes its practice a business necessity.

2.3 Grocers, Inc. is hiring cashiers. Aron is 58 and applies for a position. The HR director decides not to hire Aron, preferring someone younger, but does not give that reason to Aron. Does Aron have a claim under the ADEA for age discrimination?

A. No; Aron will never be able to prove that age was the reason for the decision.

B. No; only animus against old people is prohibited by the ADEA.

C. Yes; the decision was motivated by Aron's age.

D. Yes; employers are required to consider age as a positive factor.

**2.4** The State's veteran services office has a veteran's preference policy for hiring. Veterans au-to-matically are preferred over non-veterans, regardless of qualifications. Only 10% of veterans are women. Jane, who is not a veteran, has applied for several of these positions, but a male veteran has been awarded the position each time. If Jane, after exhausting administrative remedies, sues an appropriate State defendant for sex discrimination in an appropriate court, what is the likely outcome?

A. A win for the State because it is not an employer under Title VII.

B. A win for the State, as long as the veteran's preference is job related and consistent with business necessity.

C. A win for Jane, because the manifest imbalance of women veterans makes this disparate treatment on the basis of sex.

D. A win for Jane, because veterans are not a protected class under Title VII.

**2.5** The metropolitan area of the City of Gotham, like many cities in the U.S., has significant racial residential segregation. In the city, 40% of residents are Black, 20% are Latino, 30% are white, and about 10% are Asian. In the suburbs, 70% are white, 20% are Asian, 7% are Latino, and 3% are Black. Elm Park is a suburb that borders on the city. The hiring policy for teachers that the Elm Park school district follows has a preference for applicants who live in Elm Park. As a result, the demographics of the teachers mirror the demographics of the student body fairly closely. Ana, a Black teacher who lives outside the district, applied to the Elm Park school district but was not hired. Instead, a white applicant from Elm Park was hired.

After exhausting her administrative remedies, Ana brings a claim for race discrimination under Title VII. Which of the following statements about that claim is most correct?

A. Ana can bring this claim as both a disparate treatment claim and a disparate impact claim.

B. Ana can bring this claim as a disparate treatment claim but not a disparate impact claim.

C. Ana can bring this claim as a disparate impact claim but not a disparate treatment claim.

D. Ana cannot bring this claim as a disparate impact or disparate treatment claim.

**2.6** If instead of a public school district, the employer was a private school and Ana brings this claim under § 1981, does the answer change? Why or why not?

**2.7** If Ana brings this claim under Title VII, what is Elm Park's best defense?

A. Preferring Elm Park residents is a nondiscriminatory reason for hiring decisions because residency isn't a class protected by Title VII.

B. Local residency is a bona fide occupational qualification for the district's teachers.

C. Because the demographics of the teaching staff mirror the student body, there is no disparate impact on the basis of race.

D. Local residency is job related and consistent with business necessity for a teaching position in this community's school district.

**2.8** Advanced Technologies uses hazardous materials in some of its production processes. Some of those materials are linked with an increased risk of mutagenic effects on sperm, which can cause chromosomal abnormalities in offspring. If, to protect the offspring of male employees, Advanced Technologies adopts a policy barring fertile men from certain jobs, and they are sued under Title VII, what is their best defense?

A. Being non-fertile is a business necessity for these jobs.

B. Safety is a benign reason for making this distinction, so there is no sex-based animus, and no disparate treatment.

C. The potential cost of tort liability poses an undue hardship on the business.

D. This is one of the rare circumstances where safety to third parties justifies sex being a bona fide occupational qualification, in part because the employer did not likely adopt the policy based on stereotypical views of male workers.

**2.9** Eon Corp. is located in a metro area that has significant residential segregation. Residents of the city are more likely to be Black or Latino, while residents of the suburbs are more likely to be white. Eon Corp. is located in an office park in one of the suburbs. Over time, it has determined that employees who live in the same zip code as the company tend to be the best employees and stay with the company longer. As a result, it adopts a hiring policy preferring applicants whose home addresses are within that zip code. If Eon Corp. is sued for race discrimination under Title VII, what defense is available to it?

A. Preferring applicants by zip codes is job related and consistent with business necessity.

B. Zip codes are a reasonable factor other than race.

C. Eon Corp.'s data shows that zip codes are bona fide occupational qualifications for it.

D. Accommodating applicants from other zip codes would be unreasonable.

# Disparate Treatment, the *McDonnell Douglas* Test, and other Frameworks

3.1 When an employer comes forward with a nondiscriminatory reason for its action, the presumption of discrimination drops out of the picture. What does the Supreme Court say the effect of this is?

A. The presumption drops out, but a permissible inference of discrimination remains and can support a finding of discrimination if the employer's reason is not believed.

B. No inference of discrimination remains, and the plaintiff has to use other evidence to affirmatively demonstrate discrimination.

C. The plaintiff loses, and judgment is entered.

D. The plaintiff may still prevail, but can't be awarded damages.

3.2 If the employer comes forward with a nondiscriminatory reason, but the plaintiff provides enough evidence that the trier of fact disbelieves that it was the real reason, what happens?

A. The trier of fact must find for the plaintiff because a lie is no evidence at all.

B. The trier of fact must find for the defendant unless the plaintiff has affirmatively shown that his or her protected class was the real reason for the adverse action.

C. The trier of fact may find for the plaintiff with no more evidence than the prima facie case and the proof that the reason given wasn't the real reason.

D. The trier of fact must find for the defendant unless there is direct evidence of discrimination.

3.3 What is the only procedural stage in litigation where a defendant can challenge the plaintiff's prima facie case—argue that the plaintiff has not made one?

A. A motion to dismiss.

B. A motion for summary judgment.

C. A motion for directed verdict at the close of all the evidence.

D. A motion to set aside a jury verdict.

**3.4** Ellis is one of only 3 Latino workers at Package Express. His job is to drive a truck and deliver packages. He is assigned a delivery territory and must average delivery of 50 packages per day. Up until a month ago, his territory centered around his house and extended about an hour's drive in each direction. Most days, he could deliver 50 packages within about 8 hours, although sometimes he had to work a little longer. A month ago, his territory was extended, so that now it takes him 9 hours on average to deliver 50 packages. The reason given for the change was that his Latino heritage made him a harder worker, and so he could handle the extra driving. Ellis sued in an appropriate court after exhausting his administrative remedies. Package Express has moved for summary judgment on the ground that Ellis cannot produce evidence that he suffered an adverse employment action. What is the likely result?

A. A denial of summary judgment because the hours of work are likely a term, condition, or privilege of employment.

B. A denial of summary judgment because there is direct evidence that Package Express relied on Ellis's race or national origin to make the change to his route.

C. A grant of summary judgment because the number of packages Ellis is required to deliver remained the same.

D. A grant of summary judgment because Title VII only protects decisions about hiring, firing, promotions, pay, and discipline.

**3.5** In both *Patterson v. McLean Credit Union*, 491 U.S. 164 (1989), and *Ash v. Tyson Foods*, 546 U.S. 454 (2006), the Supreme Court considered comparator evidence. What exactly is comparator evidence?

A. Evidence about how the employer acted in a similar situation before.

B. Evidence about how the employer treated someone similarly situated to the plaintiff.

C. Evidence about whether the employer followed its own procedures.

D. Evidence about how qualified an employee is.

**3.6** Both *Patterson v. McLean Credit Union*, 491 U.S. 164 (1989), and *Ash v. Tyson Foods*, 546 U.S. 454 (2006), were promotion cases, but the principles would apply more broadly. When a plaintiff is using qualifications evidence to challenge an employer decision, which of the following is the most accurate statement of the law?

A. The plaintiff must demonstrate that he or she is so much more qualified that the disparity in qualifications is so apparent as "virtually to jump off the page and slap you in the face."

B. The plaintiff must demonstrate that he or she is substantially more qualified, to raise an inference of discrimination.

C. The plaintiff must demonstrate that he or she is qualified, but may demonstrate that whatever reason the employer gives is not the true reason in many ways, not limited to qualifications evidence.

D. Evidence that the plaintiff is more qualified will never be enough by itself to get to a jury.

**3.7** The plaintiff in *Reeves v. Sanderson Plumbing Products, Inc.*, 530 U.S. 133 (2000), had evidence to show a prima facie case and enough evidence that the trier of fact could disbelieve the reason the employer gave for firing him. A jury found in his favor and awarded him damages. Why did the Court of Appeals reverse?

A. Because the employer had a non-age-related reason for the termination.

B. Because, even though the plaintiff proved that the reason given wasn't the real reason, he did not have enough evidence that made age the inescapable reason (proof of pretext plus something else to show age).

C. Because the plaintiff couldn't find a comparator outside of his protected class.

D. Because there was no direct evidence of age discrimination.

**3.8** In *McDonald v. Santa Fe Trail Transportation Co.*, 427 U.S. 273 (1976), four employees, three Black men and one white man, stole some antifreeze from their employer. The plaintiff, the white man, was terminated for this, but the Black men were not. Ordinarily, theft would be a good reason to terminate an employee. Why did the Court nonetheless hold that race discrimination might have occurred?

A. The comparator evidence suggested that race, rather than the theft, was the reason for the termination.

B. The value of the antifreeze created only a de minimis injury to the employer.

C. Penalizing this theft caused a disparate impact against the white employee.

D. Because only one employee was terminated, penalizing theft was not a business necessity in this context.

**3.9** Ann applied to be partner. Some decisionmakers voted to deny her the promotion because she was not feminine enough. Other decisionmakers voted to deny her the promotion because she was mean to support staff. Is the firm likely to be liable for sex discrimination?

A. No. Because some decisionmakers relied on her behavior with support staff, the firm had a legitimate nondiscriminatory reason for its actions.

B. No. Partners are not employees, and so she was no longer covered by Title VII.

C. Yes. As long as sex was a motivating factor, the firm will be liable for discrimination.

D. Yes. Ann's treatment of support staff was not a legitimate reason for the promotion decision.

**3.10** If some partners instead thought that Ann was too old, how would the answer change?

**3.11** Fred applied for a job with Workplace, Inc., but he was not hired. He is Black, and Workplace, Inc. has very few Black employees—only about 1%. Fred had the minimum qualifications and so did the white man who was eventually hired for the position. During the interview, Fred was asked whether he would feel isolated as one of the few Black employees. He answered that he would not, that he had gone to school at primarily white institutions, and that he was used to working with, primarily, white people. Fred exhausted his administrative remedies and brought an action in an appropriate court against Workplace. At the close of evidence, Workplace moves for a directed verdict. What is the likely result?

A. Denial. Looking at the evidence as a whole, a reasonable jury could conclude that the decisionmaker was motivated by race.

B. Denial. Because there is a manifest imbalance on the basis of race within Workplace's workforce, Fred is entitled to have the jury decide.

C. Grant. Because Fred can't prove he was more qualified than the person chosen, he cannot make a prima facie case of discrimination.

D. Grant. Fred has no evidence that Workplace has lied about anything and so cannot prove pretext.

**3.12** Evelyn has a difficult relationship with her supervisor. Evelyn's supervisor cannot stand the fact that Evelyn is an atheist. The supervisor criticizes Evelyn whenever she can on pretextual grounds, hoping that Evelyn will be fired. Evelyn's supervisor has no power to fire Evelyn or otherwise discipline her, but the supervisor's notes are part of the file that Mel, the manager, uses to make employment decisions. Based on the supervisor's notes, Mel fires Evelyn, believing her to be incompetent. If, after Evelyn exhausts her administrative remedies, she sues in an appropriate court, what is the likely result?

A. A loss for Evelyn because the decisionmaker believed in good faith that Evelyn was a bad employee.

B. A loss for Evelyn because atheism is not protected by Title VII.

C. A win for Evelyn because her supervisor coerced her based on religion.

D. A win for Evelyn as long as the supervisor's notes were the proximate cause of her discharge.

**3.13** Finn is non-binary and was passed over for a promotion. Finn exhausted their administrative remedies and filed a complaint under Title VII in an appropriate federal court. That complaint alleged that Finn had all of the qualifications that the employer advertised for the promotion but that Finn was not promoted. Finn also alleged that in the past, coworkers had made derogatory comments about Finn's non-binary gender, and that when Finn complained, the HR Director told Finn to just ignore them. Finn also alleged that their manager had misgendered them on several occasions and reacted defensively when Finn corrected that. The decisionmakers for the promotion decision were the HR Director and Finn's manager.

The employer has moved to dismiss the complaint on the ground that the allegations are not framed to satisfy the prima facie case standard established in *McDonnell Douglas v. Green,* 411 U.S. 792 (1973). How will the court likely rule?

A. Motion granted. Without direct evidence of discrimination, a plaintiff must use the *McDonnell Douglas* burden-shifting framework.

B. Motion granted. Every jurisdiction requires comparator evidence.

C. Motion denied. A complaint need not plead elements of the *McDonnell Douglas* burden shifting framework even in a circumstantial case.

D. Motion denied. The employer failed to articulate its nondiscriminatory reason for not promoting Finn in its motion to dismiss, and so failed to satisfy its burden.

**3.14** Grace has worked at Hobbystore for years. She has generally received positive reviews and gotten along well with her coworkers. She recently notified her supervisor that she is pregnant and will be taking some leave when the baby is born. After this, her supervisor started treating her differently, complaining about her work, and giving her less desirable assignments. About two weeks before Grace's due date, she was terminated. The reason given by Hobbystore was that they were restructuring the department Grace was in. After the baby was born, Grace went shopping at Hobbystore, and noticed that the department seemed to be staffed just like when she worked there. She filed a charge with the EEOC for discrimination on the basis of sex (pregnancy), received a right to sue letter, and filed an action in an appropriate court.

Hobbystore has filed a motion for summary judgment, arguing that Grace will not be able to prove that she was fired because of her pregnancy, providing an affidavit from Grace's supervisor that the reason Grace was fired was her poor performance. How will the court likely rule?

A. Motion denied; looking at the evidence as a whole, a factfinder could infer that Grace's pregnancy was the reason for her termination, and that the shifting reasons provided by the employer demonstrate pretext.

B. Motion denied; employers who terminate pregnant workers so close to their due date are presumed to be discriminating.

C. Motion granted unless Grace can provide evidence of a non-pregnant comparator.

D. Motion granted; the supervisor's affidavit that Grace's work suffered is consistent with how she treated Grace before Grace was terminated, so Grace will be unable to demonstrate pretext.

Topic 4 **Questions**

# Defense to Disparate Treatment: BFOQ

4.1 Zhang Wei is the owner and sole proprietor of a Chinese restaurant in South County that employs thirty people. Wei wants to establish a dining experience authentic to mainland China and so only hires kitchen staff born in mainland China.

Juan, a chef born in the United States with Latino heritage, applies for a kitchen position. Wei refuses to hire him because he was not born in mainland China. If Juan sues Wei for discrimination, what is the likely result?

A. A loss, because Chinese heritage is a business necessity for an authentic Chinese restaurant.

B. A loss because the ability to cook authentic Chinese food is a bona fide occupational qualification.

C. A win, because Title VII prohibits national origin discrimination.

D. A win, because Wei and Juan are of different races, and race cannot be a BFOQ.

4.2 On average, women have less upper body strength than men do. Because firefighters have to carry heavy equipment, the fire department only hires men to be firefighters. If a female candidate brings an action in an appropriate court, what is the likely result?

A. A win for the candidate because sex is not a BFOQ for fighting fires or performing rescues.

B. A win for the candidate because strength is not a business necessity for all firefighting activities.

C. A loss for the candidate because public safety makes upper body strength a BFOQ.

D. A loss for the candidate because the link between sex and strength is a real difference and not a prescriptive stereotype.

4.3 A national massage chain hires only female masseuses. It has extensive data showing that both men and women tend to prefer massages by women for reasons of privacy; the person being massaged is often naked. If a male masseur brings an appropriate action, what is the likely result?

A. A win for the masseur because no constitutional privacy interests are at stake.

B. A win for the masseur because customer preference cannot make sex a BFOQ.

C. A loss for the masseur because privacy is a BFOQ.

D. A loss for the masseur because the chain is motivated by privacy concerns and not sex.

**4.4** Lead poses risks to workers and to fetuses in utero. Because of this risk, Battery Co. prohibits women of reproductive age from working in the parts of the plant that have high lead exposure. Battery Co. is sued by a class of women. Is Battery Co. likely to be liable for its conduct?

A. No, because safety can make sex a BFOQ, and Battery Co. only wants to protect its women employees.

B. No, because safety to third parties can make sex a BFOQ, and Battery Co. only wants to protect the fetuses of women employees.

C. Yes, because working safely does not go to the essence of the business of making batteries.

D. Yes, because the category of workers protected was overbroad.

**4.5** Babbleberry sells women's clothes. It hires only female models for advertisements. If a male model brings an appropriate action challenging this practice, what is the likely result?

A. A loss for Babbleberry because sex is not relevant to a person's ability to be photogenic.

B. A loss for Babbleberry because people of all genders wear clothes.

C. A win for Babbleberry because the target market of female customers brings this practice within the authenticity exception for a BFOQ.

D. A win for Bableberry because modelling is not covered by Title VII.

**4.6** Hooters and other "breastaurants" (that's the industry term) hire only women to be servers. What is Hooters' best argument that sex is a BFOQ for its business?

**4.7** Which of the following is most likely to be considered a BFOQ?

A. Hiring only women to be gestational surrogates.

B. Hiring only women to sell cosmetics.

C. Hiring only men to be correctional officers at a men's prison.

D. Hiring only men to be professional football players.

Topic 5 Questions

# Conduct-Based Disparate Treatment: Retaliation

5.1 Jack was accused of sexual harassment by his subordinate Jenna. She sued their employer, and Jack insisted on taking the stand to testify about what happened, saying that he had not engaged in the conduct she accused him of. A jury found in favor of the employer. After the verdict, the employer fired Jack, stating that his insistence on taking the stand disrupted the office.

If Jack, after pursuing the appropriate administrative actions, sues the employer, what is the likely outcome?

A. A win for Jack because Title VII protects men from sex discrimination, too.

B. A win for Jack because he was fired for participating in proceedings under Title VII.

C. A win for the employer because it has a legitimate interest in preventing sexual harassment.

D. A win for the employer because testifying for the defense does not qualify as opposing discrimination in proceedings under Title VII.

5.2 Aron experienced harassment from a supervisor at work. As part of the employer's internal harassment investigation against that supervisor in response to complaint from a different employee, Aron was interviewed and shared the harassing experiences, describing them in negative terms. Based on that interview, Aron was fired. If Aron brings an action for retaliation in an appropriate court, what is the likely result?

A. A win for Aron because sharing negative information about harassment is protected opposition conduct.

B. A win for Aron because the interview was protected by the proceedings clause of Title VII's retaliation provision.

C. A loss for Aron because Aron did not volunteer the information before the investigation.

D. A loss for Aron because this is a third-party retaliation claim.

**5.3** Bell complained to management about a racial pay gap at the company. In response to the complaint, management removed Bell from a party-planning committee at work, stating that employees that complain don't get rewarded. That committee planned monthly parties to celebrate the birthdays of every employee with a birthday in that month. It did not come with any extra pay or time off, but it was considered a fun thing to do. If Bell challenges the removal as retaliation under Title VII, what is the likely result?

A. A loss for the employer as long as Bell believed in good faith that a racial pay gap violates Title VII.

B. A loss for the employer because any negative change in working conditions violates Title VII's anti-retaliation provision.

C. A win for the employer because removal from a voluntary committee, even a fun one, likely would not deter a reasonable employee from complaining about discrimination.

D. A win for the employer because the ability to serve on the committee was not a term or condition of employment.

**5.4** Sara, a supervisor at Shopway, fired Cary, a cashier, because Cary was a Jehovah's witness. Sara lied and said Cary was terminated for misconduct. To cover herself, Sara wrote up a false disciplinary note for Cary's file and backdated it to a few weeks before the termination. Cary sued under Title VII, and Sara testified for the employer. Cary was able to prove at trial that Sara lied and created the false note. Shopway's manager wants to fire Sara for discriminating and lying and asks the HR Director if they can legally do that. What should the HR Director say?

A. No, because testifying is protected by the proceedings clause, and proceedings clause protection is nearly absolute.

B. No, because Sara was the employer's witness, and not an opposition witness.

C. Yes, because Sara's agreement to participate in the trial when she knew she might have to commit perjury violated the duty of loyalty she owed Shopway.

D. Yes, because the reason for the discharge is the discrimination and cover up, not the fact of Sara's testimony.

**5.5** Adam and Ben are Black men, working at Organics, a large grocery chain. In the summer of 2020, Organics had a mask mandate in effect for its stores, to guard against the spread of COVID-19. Adam and Ben wore masks that said, "Black Lives Matter" in solidarity with the movement for racial justice. Organics allowed masks with slogans and statements, including masks that included things like a flag with a thin blue line, a controversial symbol in support of law enforcement, and statements like, "Italian and Proud." It fired Adam and Ben, though, on the grounds that their masks were divisive. Carl and Dave, white coworkers of Adam and Ben, began wearing Black Lives Matter masks after the firing, protesting Organics' actions, which they believed were racially discriminatory. They too were fired for wearing the masks. If, after exhausting their administrative remedies, all four men bring a Title VII retaliation claim against Organics, what is the likely result?

A. A win for all four men because wearing the masks was protected opposition conduct.

B. A win only for Carl and Dave because their actions were protected opposition conduct while Adam and Ben's actions were not.

C. A win only for Adam and Ben because they were more affected by racism as Black men, so only their conduct was protected opposition conduct.

D. A loss for all four men because political speech is not protected by Title VII.

**5.6** Evan and Frankie are coworkers and close friends. When Evan experienced discrimination, he filed a charge with the EEOC, alleging a violation of Title VII. The employer fired Frankie, telling him that the reason was Evan's charge and a fear that Frankie would make trouble on Evan's behalf. Can Frankie bring an action against the employer for retaliation under Title VII?

A. No, Frankie didn't participate in the proceedings, and it doesn't seem that he did anything to oppose discrimination, either.

B. No, Title VII doesn't protect coworkers from retaliation.

C. Yes, Frankie's relationship with Evan made the employer fear protected opposition conduct.

D. Yes, if Evan and Frankie's relationship was close enough that the employer's action would deter a reasonable employee in Evan's position from filing a charge.

**5.7** Glen was viewed as something of a trouble maker by her employer. She was always complaining that the employer's dress code was discriminatory because it prohibited open-toed shoes, and women's shoes are often open-toed. She even filed a charge with the EEOC about it. Glen also had trouble getting along with her co-workers. She was difficult, sometimes yelling in the office about whose turn it was to bring the coffee, telling her coworkers they were bad at their jobs, and sending rude emails. Finally, Glen's employer had enough and fired her, stating that her constant troublemaking and even getting the EEOC involved was damaging morale. If Glen brings a retaliation action against the employer, what is the likely result?

A. A win for the employer because, at worst, its motives for firing Glen were mixed.

B. A win for the employer but only if it can prove it would have taken the same action without considering the EEOC charge.

C. A win for Glen because the employer admitted it was motivated in part by her EEOC charge.

D. A win for Glen as long as a reasonable person would think that the dress code policy violated Title VII.

# Systemic Disparate Treatment

6.1 Bigbox Shopping is a general merchandise retailer in Philadelphia. There are essentially three types of jobs at Bigbox: stocking jobs, cashiers, and management. Stockers mostly work in the stockroom, out of sight of customers. Cashiers, sell the merchandise to the customers. And management supervises both. Philadelphia is a pretty diverse city. About 44% of people are white, 44% are Black, about 8% are Asian, and the remaining 4%, Latino. 80% of the stockers are Black, while 90% of the cashiers are white. And out of 20 supervisory/management employees, only 1 is non-white, a Latino man. The EEOC brought a pattern and practice case against Bigbox. At trial, it presented this demographic evidence and evidence from several Black applicants for cashier positions, who were told that they would probably be more comfortable in stocker positions instead. At the close of the EEOC's case, Bigbox moved for a directed verdict in its favor.

How should the court rule?

A. Deny the motion because pattern and practice cases are governed by a different provision within Title VII than the usual enforcement provision.

B. Deny the motion because the statistical evidence plus anecdotal evidence are sufficient to make a prima facie case of a pattern and practice of discrimination.

C. Grant the motion because the EEOC has not provided direct evidence of discrimination.

D. Grant the motion because, while the EEOC has proven a prima facie case, it has not provided evidence of pretext.

6.2 If the EEOC proves that an employer has engaged in a pattern and practice of discrimination, what defenses are available to that employer?

6.3 Roebucks is a national department store that sells a wide variety of things from clothes and cosmetics to power tools and appliances. Employees who sell clothes are paid on an hourly basis, while those who sell power tools and appliances are paid on a commission basis. Employees paid on a commission basis make more, generally, than those paid on an hourly basis. Hourly employees are almost all women, while commission sellers are almost all men. Roebucks has tried to recruit women to its commission sales positions, but it has not seen a lot of success. It has also surveyed its employees about their job satisfaction, and 75% of hourly employees reported that they were satisfied with their jobs and would not want to move into a commission sales position.

If the EEOC brings a pattern and practice claim against Roebucks for sex discrimination, pointing out the large pay disparity, what is Robucks's best defense?

A. No statistical analysis can possibly account for all of the factors that result in this disparity.

B. Hiring men for commission sales work is a business necessity because of the nature of the products sold.

C. Hiring men for commission sales work is a BFOQ because men are better at selling power tools and appliances.

D. The sex-based disparity is caused by women's lack of interest and not discrimination by Roebucks.

**6.4** Hugeco is a large, national discount store with about 1 million employees. About ⅔ of its entry-level employees are women, about ⅔ of its mid-level managers are men, and about 98% of its higher-level managers are men. Hugeco promotes from within. It doesn't advertise openings, but instead, current managers encourage those they supervise to apply when openings occur. After exhausting their administrative remedies, a class of all women who work at Hugeco brings an action against it for sex discrimination in promotions. At trial, they present statistical evidence that shows a substantial disparity nationwide on the basis of sex. They also present six instances where women who asked about promotions were told that they likely weren't eligible because the new position would require travel, which moms shouldn't do. What is Hugeco's best defense?

A. Six instances of disparate treatment are not sufficient in connection with the statistical evidence to show a pattern of discriminatory decisions nationwide.

B. Comments like that are only stray remarks in such a large workplace and can't be attributed to the company.

C. The promotional policy is not discriminatory because supervisors are in the best position to see who would be most qualified for a promotion.

D. The lack of interest defense rebuts any inference of discrimination here.

# Disparate Impact

7.1 Sara is a Black woman who has worked at City Bank for five years as a teller. She is the Bank's only Black employee. Over the last two years, there have been three openings for supervisory positions, and Sara applied for all three. Each time, a white teller with the same qualifications and similar levels of experience was promoted. There are no set standards for promotion; the bank's managers simply decide who they think would be a good fit. After exhausting her administrative remedies, Sara brought a disparate impact action under Title VII for race discrimination against the bank.

If the bank moves to dismiss Sara's claim, what is the likely result?

A. A win for the bank. Because the bank used no test or credential to make its decision, the decision can only be challenged using the disparate treatment framework.

B. A win for the bank. The number of promotion decisions is too few to show a racial disparity.

C. A loss for the bank. Wholly subjective decisionmaking processes can be challenged using disparate impact.

D. A loss for the bank. Wholly subjective decisionmaking processes are per se discriminatory because of implicit bias.

7.2 What made the Court conclude in *Griggs v. Duke Power Co.*, 401 U.S. 424 (1971), that the diploma requirement and the tests were not job related?

7.3 In *Dothard v. Rawlinson*, 433 U.S. 321 (1977), the Court held that a requirement that excluded 41% of the female population but excluded less than 1% of the male population created a disparate impact on the basis of sex. Why did Justice White critique this analysis?

**7.4** In *New York City Transit Authority v. Beazer*, 440 U.S. 568 (1979), the Court rejected a claim that the Transit Authority's anti-narcotics policy, which excluded anyone on a methadone maintenance program, caused a disparate impact on Black and Hispanic employees and applicants. The district court had found that 81% of the employees referred to the medical director for suspected violation of the narcotics rule were Black or Hispanic and that about 63% of people on methadone maintenance programs were Black or Hispanic. Why didn't those statistics show a disparate impact?

**7.5** In *New York City Transit Authority v. Beazer*, 440 U.S. 568 (1979), what was Justice White's critique of the majority's Title VII analysis?

**7.6** What is the difference between applicant pool data and applicant flow data?

**7.7** Company Corp. is hiring employees and gives a test as part of that hiring process. 75 applicants took the test. 50 of these are white, and 25 are Black. 37 applicants passed the test. 25 were white, and 12 were Black. Did the test cause a disparate impact on the basis of race?

**7.8** *Connecticut v. Teal*, 457 U.S. 440 (1982), involved a disparate impact challenge to a promotion process that had two steps. Applicants took a test, and if they passed, were deemed eligible, but not automatically promoted. The hiring committee chose who to promote from those who passed the test, applying an affirmative action plan. Do the math to see why the plaintiffs alleged an unlawful disparate impact and why the defendant argued that there was no disparate impact.

Total number of applicants/test takers: 329

Total number of applicants/test takers identifying as Black: 48

Total number of applicants/test takers identifying as white: 259 (7 were Hispanic & 15 were unidentified)

White test passers: 206

Black test passers: 26

White applicants promoted (the affirmative action step): 35

Black applicants promoted: 11

Calculate the rates of promotion for Black applicants (from application to promotion) and white applicants, and then compare the success rates of black to white applicants.

Calculate the rates of test passage for Black applicants and white applicants and compare the success rates of black to white applicants

Do either of these show a disparate impact on the basis of race? What were the arguments made about what calculation mattered?

7.9 Chicago Lamp employs 5,000 people. It is surrounded by a multicultural neighborhood with the following racial composition: 50% African American, 30% Latino, 10% Asian, and 10% Caucasian. There are no special skills involved in putting together the streetlights manufactured by the company. Most of the workers (approximately 90%) are Asian, and so are the owners of the company. The owners of the company do not advertise for workers. Instead, they hire new employees by telling their current workers to bring their friends to an "open hiring call." Can an appropriate plaintiff bring a disparate impact claim against the company?

A. No; there is no neutral practice to point to.

B. No; the workers could have friends of any race, and there is no demographic data on who attends these open hiring calls.

C. Yes; it's unlikely that this method of recruitment is job related and consistent with a business necessity.

D. Yes; the resulting disparity speaks for itself.

7.10 Babble is a web service that is growing quickly and needs to hire programmers. The hiring process requires applicants to do a coding project and have a 5 minute speed-dating-type interview. Neither of these things are given scores, but the committee ranks applicants after both things, looking at each applicant "as a whole person" and their code "based on both functionality and elegance." Fifty people applied, and ten were hired. The demographics of the applicant pool were: 20 people who were Asian descent, 15 people who were white, 10 people who were Black, and 5 people who were Latino. From that group, 6 hired were Asian, and the other 4 were white. If a Black and Latino applicant sue for disparate impact, can their claim get past a motion to dismiss?

A. Yes; because the hiring process led to a disparate impact on the basis of race.

B. Yes; because stereotypes are clearly driving the subjective interview process.

C. No; because the plaintiffs can't point to which portion of the hiring process caused the disparate impact.

D. No; because the majority of those hired were from a racial minority group.

# Defenses to Disparate Impact

8.1 True or false: Even if individual steps in the hiring process cause a disparate impact, an employer will not be liable for discrimination if the process as a whole does not.

8.2 In *Griggs v. Duke Power Co.*, 401 U.S. 424 (1971), the employer required employees who wanted to move into three of the four main units of the plant to have a high school diploma and pass two professionally developed tests. Why were those requirements discriminatory?

A. Because they were adopted as a way to keep Black employees concentrated in the lowest paying positions.

B. Because they were not professionally developed tests created for this workplace.

C. Because Black applicants were much less likely to have a diploma or pass the tests, and those requirements were not clearly job related.

D. Because adopting these requirements changed the settled expectations of the workers.

8.3 The City of Townsville Police Department (CTPD) uses a two-step process for determining whether to promote individuals in its organization from rank-and-file employees to supervisors. The first part of the process is a professionally developed test. The test accurately covers knowledge essential for the job of supervisors, and those with the highest scores in the past have gotten more positive performance reviews. Fifty men and 50 women take the promotion test. 80% of men pass (40), but only 40% of women pass (20). From the resulting eligibility list, CTPD then engages in individual interviews to determine who will receive the promotion. After the interviews, 6 men (12% of men who had applied for promotion) and 6 women (12% of women who had applied for promotion) are chosen for the twelve promotions.

A group of women, who failed the test and did not get promoted, bring a disparate impact claim for sex discrimination. Will their claims be successful?

A. No, because the test is valid.

B. No, because § 703(h) of Title VII explicitly provides that it "shall [not] be an unlawful employment practice for an employer to give and to act upon the results of any professionally developed ability test . . . ."

C. Yes, because the test presumptively caused a disparate impact on women since they passed at a rate less than 4/5ths of the rate at which men passed.

D. Yes, because failing to get rid of the test with a disparate impact was itself disparate treatment.

8.4 In *Wards Cove v. Atonio*, 490 U.S. 642 (1989), the Court reversed a lower court finding of disparate impact liability. In that case, the salmon cannery workforce was highly racially stratified. Cannery jobs were filled primarily by Filipinos and Alaska natives, while non-cannery jobs were filled by white workers. Why wasn't that extreme racial segregation evidence of discrimination?

A. Statistical proof alone cannot make out a prima facie case of disparate impact discrimination.

B. The cannery work force was not the qualified labor pool for non-cannery jobs.

C. The subjective employment criteria used by the company could not be challenged on a disparate impact theory.

D. The objective criteria were clearly job related.

8.5 Happy Housekeepers is a company that provides housecleaning services. After it received a few complaints about the quality of work by some of its employees it decided to institute a new requirement for hirees. The complaints were, generally, that the house cleaners had not been as thorough as the homeowners would have liked. The new requirement was that housecleaners would have to have a bachelor's degree. The company thought that might result in a better class of worker. The new requirement of a bachelor's degree has a disparate impact on the basis of national origin. If the EEOC brings an action against the company, what is the likely result?

A. A loss for the EEOC unless a sufficient number of applicants filed charges based on this employment practice.

B. A loss for the EEOC because the disparity in bachelor's degrees is not something Title VII can redress.

C. A win for the EEOC because it does not appear that the employer did a job analysis or that having a bachelor's degree would be correlated with the job or skill at being a thorough cleaner.

D. A win for the EEOC because having a bachelor's degree for this type of service position would not be a bona fide occupational qualification.

Topic 9 Questions

# Harassment

9.1 Fran is Black woman with a white supervisor, who has the power to fire her. Last week, Fran's supervisor used a race-based epithet in her presence. If Fran brings an action in an appropriate court and the employer wins at trial, what is the most likely reason?

A. Because the supervisor's conduct was not sexual in nature, it did not violate Title VII.

B. Only tangible employment actions are actionable in harassment claims.

C. Harassment is outside the scope of a supervisor's job duties and so an employer cannot be liable for the supervisor's actions.

D. While the conduct was arguably severe, it was not pervasive enough to create a hostile work environment.

9.2 Glen's supervisor makes comments every day for a year about Glen's body, like, "Hubba, hubba. Aren't you fit?" and, "You have clearly been lifting." The supervisor does not make those comments to workers of any other sex. If Glen brings an action in an appropriate court and the employer wins at trial, what is the most likely reason?

A. These are simply stray comments in the workplace and cannot, as a matter of law, create an inference of sexual harassment.

B. While the comments were arguably pervasive, the conduct was not severe enough to that a reasonable employee would find this an abusive workplace.

C. Unless Glen was constructively discharged, there can be no actionable harassment claim.

D. There was no demand that Glen submit to sexual advances, which is necessary for a sexual harassment claim.

9.3 When Mel applied for a promotion at work, Mel's supervisor, the decisionmaker, said, "If you sleep with me, the promotion is yours." Mel slept with the supervisor and was promoted. Despite the company's well-known harassment policy, Mel did not report the supervisor to management. If Mel sues the employer for harassment, what is the likely result?

A. A win for Mel because the promotion was a tangible employment action.

B. A win for Mel because the sexual advance created a hostile environment.

C. A loss for Mel because Mel was promoted, so there was no injury.

D. A loss for Mel because Mel unreasonably failed to follow the employer's harassment policy and report the advance.

**9.4** Hugeco has a comprehensive, clear policy forbidding sexual harassment. Although Hugeco sees itself as a progressive, employee-friendly employer, Emma Employee doesn't see things that way. Indeed, Emma claims that the sexual harassment that she has suffered at the hands of her supervisor, Sam, has given her no choice but to quit her employment and that any reasonable person would have felt the same way. Emma did not complain of the harassment to others in the company before quitting. Assuming Emma can make out the other elements of her sexual harassment claim, will she be able to hold Hugeco liable for the sexual harassment by Sam?

A. Yes, if her choice to quit was precipitated by some official act Sam took that only a supervisor could take.

B. No, because she quit. She wasn't fired.

C. Yes, because employers are always liable for the conduct of supervisors.

D. Not likely, because Hugeco will have an affirmative defense that its policy was a reasonable way to prevent and remedy harassment and Emma's failure to report the harassment was unreasonable.

**9.5** If Emma's supervisor lacked the power to hire or fire her, what would she have to prove to hold Hugeco liable?

**9.6** Frank has worked for Widget Corporation for 10 years and had good reviews. He got a new supervisor a couple of months ago. His new supervisor, who had the power to fire him, began scrutinizing his work more closely than his prior supervisor had, and in the last month, started making comments about Frank's race in connection with his performance. Frank reported the supervisor's comments to management, and the supervisor was transferred. Frank hasn't experienced further harassment. If Frank brings an action under Title VII against his employer what is the likely result?

A. A win for Frank because Frank promptly reported the harassment.

B. A win for Frank because employers are vicariously liable for the conduct that supervisors engage in.

C. A win for Widget Co. because it acted promptly to remedy harassment it learned of.

D. A win for Widget Co. because no tangible employment action was taken against Frank.

**9.7** Imagine instead that Frank's supervisor did not have the power to fire him, Frank did not report the harassment, and it escalated. If after three months, Frank filed a charge with the EEOC, and then an action in an appropriate court, what is the likely result?

A. A win for Widget Co. because Frank never reported the harassment.

B. A win for Widget Co. unless Frank can demonstrate that the company knew or should have known of the harassment and failed to prevent or remedy it.

C. A win for Frank unless Widget Co. can demonstrate that it's antiharassment policy has been effective in other situations.

D. A win for Frank because the harassment is more likely severe or pervasive enough to have created a hostile work environment.

**9.8** Tortion motors has a harassment problem. Eve has seen several of her co-workers go through it. First they're targeted by a supervisor, then they report the harassment under Tortion's anti-harassment policy, and when that news gets around, their coworkers join in to teach that person a lesson for doing something that threatens the company. Management never seems to do anything about it. Now it's happening to Eve. Her supervisor has started propositioning her. Eve wants it to stop, but instead of going to management, she files a charge with the EEOC and then an action in an appropriate court. Tortion's defense is that it isn't liable for the harassment because Eve never reported it. Is that defense likely to succeed?

A. No, because if reporting would be futile, it is reasonable for an employee to not pursue it.

B. No, because Eve didn't suffer a tangible employment action.

C. Yes, because employees have to take advantage of an employer's processes if they exist.

D. Yes, because it is not the employer that is retaliating, but instead co-workers who aren't liable under Title VII.

**9.9** Glen is a manager at Homeworks, a national retail store that sells furniture and other domestic items. Glen has a confrontational management style to say the least. He often yells at Sue and tells her that she is a terrible worker. When she makes mistakes, he cuts her hours, and at her review, he put her on probation. Glenn also yells at Ted. Glenn tells Ted that he's never met anyone so stupid. And he gives Ted the worst jobs in the store. If Sue and Ted after exhausting their administrative remedies bring an action against Homework for hostile environment harassment under title VII what is the likely result?

A. A win for Ted and Sue because the harassing conduct is severe or pervasive.

B. A win for Sue because she suffered an adverse employment action but not for Ted because he did not.

C. A win for Homeworks because Glenn's conduct was outside of the scope of his duties.

D. A win for Homeworks because the reason for the harassment does not appear to be a class protected by Title VII.

Topic 10 Questions

# Focused Issues Related to Protected Classes: Race/Color

**10.1** What is race? Most scientists agree that race isn't really biological—that there is at least as much variation biologically among people grouped into a race as there is between different racial groups. Despite that, in what sense do we still tend to think of race as having a biological component?

**10.2** What does it mean to say that race is a social construct, and how might that complicate application of anti-discrimination law?

**10.3** In *McDonald v. Santa Fe Trail Transportation Co.*, 427 U.S. 273 (1976), the Supreme Court held that 42 U.S.C. § 1981 prohibited so-called, "reverse" race discrimination. Why did the defendant have a better argument than it would under Title VII that the plaintiffs were not protected?

A. As white people, the plaintiffs didn't have a race.

B. The language of § 1981 compares the group protected by the statute to white citizens, suggesting that the group protected by the statute must be not white.

C. The plaintiffs lacked employment contracts.

D. The plaintiffs committed serious misconduct—theft.

**10.4** How do courts define what counts as a race for purposes of § 1981?

A. Whatever was viewed as a race in the nineteenth century will be considered a race.

B. The current census categories of white (non-Hispanic), American Indian or Native Alaskan, Hispanic, African American or Black, Asian, Native Hawaiian or Pacific Islander.

C. Groups with heritage linked by large geographic areas that correspond to skin tone and other physical features: African, Asian, Native American, Hispanic, and Anglo or European.

D. Whatever expert scientific testimony reveals about a person's genes.

**10.5** Claude has a condition known as "pseudofolliculitis barbae," which describes persistent irritation and ingrown hairs caused by shaving. Inflamed papules can develop, and over time, they can cause keloid scarring. Doctors recommend that men with this condition not shave, or at least not shave closely. Over fifty percent of African American men suffer from PFB, while about fifteen percent of white men suffer from it.

He has applied to work as a salesperson at Bland, a large, national clothing store that celebrates, "All-American" youth culture. The company's personal appearance policy requires employees who have visible facial hair to be clean shaven. Customer surveys done every couple of years consistently show that customers associate a lack of facial hair with youth. On average, about 3% of customers say they would stop shopping at any Bland that had a salesperson with visible facial hair. Bland does not hire him, but says it would if he would shave.

If Claude, after pursuing the appropriate administrative process, sues Bland for race discrimination, what is the likely outcome?

A. A win for Claude because shaving is not a bona fide occupational qualification for clothing store employees.

B. A win for Claude because shaving imposes an undue burden on African American men.

C. A win for Bland because there is evidence that customer comfort is job related and consistent with a business necessity for this particular job.

D. A win for Bland because the condition isn't perfectly correlated with race: some African American men don't have the condition, and some white men do.

**10.6** In *St. Francis College v. al-Khazraji*, 481 U.S. 604 (1987), the Court considered whether discrimination against a doctor of Iraqi heritage was race discrimination for purposes of 42 U.S.C. § 1981. Was it?

A. No, because national origin is not the same as race.

B. No, because a person of Iraqi heritage is Caucasion.

C. Yes, because race was more like national origin or ethnic heritage at the time that § 1981 was passed.

D. Yes, because a person of Iraqi heritage is not Caucasion.

**10.7** Rebecca, a Black woman, wears her hair in a short, Afro style. She applies to work as a flight attendant at Skyhigh Airways. Skyhigh's dress code requires female flight attendants' hair to be worn straight or pinned up. When Rebecca says she won't straighten her hair, Skyhigh responds that unless she wears a wig, it will not hire her. If Rebecca brings an appropriate action against Skyhigh, what is the likely result?

A. A win for Rebecca because the dress code policy as applied discriminates on the basis of race.

B. A win for Rebecca because employers may not dictate matters of personal appearance.

C. A loss for Rebecca because hairstyle can be changed, and thus is not immutable.

D. A loss for Rebecca because the grooming code does not mention race.

**10.8** Cary is white and his spouse is Black. They live in a predominantly Black neighborhood. Cary applied for a position at Grecko, an insurance company. He had a great interview and was hired. On his first day at work, Cary filled out forms for benefits, and the HR director noticed his address. She looked surprised and asked him why he lived in that neighborhood. Cary explained both that he liked the neighborhood for its multicultural vibe and that his spouse felt more comfortable there where there were more Black and brown people. A couple of hours later, Cary's manager called him in, and broke the bad news, saying, "It looks like things aren't going to work out after all. We have to let you go." When Cary asked why, the manager said, "We're just a little concerned that your background is a lot more urban than we expected. We don't think you'll be a good fit with our suburban clientele." Cary interpreted "urban" to refer to Blackness. It is often used as code for minority groups and minority-dominant neighborhoods.

If Cary brings an action under Title VII for race discrimination after exhausting his administrative remedies, and Grecko moves to dismiss, what is the likely result?

A. A win for Grecko. Cary is white, and white people can't bring race discrimination claims.

B. A win for Grecko because the language was too coded for a reasonable factfinder to infer that race was the reason for Cary's termination.

C. A win for Cary because a reasonable jury could find that Grecko discriminated against him because of his association with Black people.

D. A win for Cary because questions of motive are fact-specific, and so must go to a jury.

**10.9** Diana is Elisha's supervisor. Both are Black women. Elisha used to straighten her hair, but she has grown tired of the cost and pain (from the chemical and heat processes) that doing so requires and to the damage to her hair, and so she has decided to get braids to transition until her hair can grow out to a more natural style. After she came to work in braids, Diana told Elisha that she looked "ghetto," and the company wouldn't stand for that. Elisha refused to change her hair. Two weeks later, Diana fired Elisha for failing to conform to a professional appearance at work.

If, after exhausting her administrative remedies, Elisha files a Title VII action against her employer, what is the likely result?

A. A win for Elisha unless the grooming code specifically prohibited braids.

B. A win for Elisha because Diana seemed to be motivated by Elisha's performance of racial identity.

C. A win for the employer because Diana and Elisha are members of the same race, and so Diana's decision cannot be racially motivated.

D. A win for the employer because hairstyles are mutable.

**10.10** The Florida House is an upscale, high-volume American seafood restaurant, somewhat famous nationally. It serves upwards of 2000 diners a night, relying on menu items that can be prepared in 15-minutes or less, and a highly organized restaurant staff of 200 employees. Darius, a dark-skinned Black man, applied to work as a server at the restaurant. He has significant experience as a server, and that position pays more than kitchen positions do. Darius was hired, but for a kitchen position. Over the course of his first few weeks, Darius noticed that many of his coworkers were Black, and there were Black employees in all roles in the restaurant. One thing struck him as odd, though. All of the Black waitstaff and employees in other front-of-house roles were lighter skinned, while all of the Black employees in back-of-house roles, including the kitchen, were darker skinned. As new people were hired, he noted the continuing pattern, that darker skinned people would be hired for back-of-house jobs, while lighter skinned people were hired for front-of-house jobs, regardless of what positions they applied for.

If, after exhausting his administrative remedies, Darius files an action challenging this practice under Title VII, what is the likely result?

A. A win for the restaurant because there is no evidence that it is discriminating on the basis of race, since Black people are hired for just about every role at the restaurant.

B. A win for the restaurant because Darius was hired and has not been fired, so has not experienced an ultimate employment action to bring an action over.

C. A win for Darius as long as he can present expert testimony about the demographics of the labor pool in the area.

D. A win for Darius because a reasonable factfinder could conclude that the restaurant is discriminating on the basis of color based on the pattern that Darius observed.

**10.11** You are a supervisor in an office. One of your direct reports is a young Black woman who has just told you that she is expecting a baby. In congratulating her, you make small talk about names, and other things common to the excitement surrounding new babies. She mentions the names she is thinking about, and one of them is Lakisha. Because you are well educated on matters of employment discrimination, you know about a famous article called, *Are Emily and Greg More Employable than Lakisha and Jamal?* That article documented the way that people with "Black-sounding" names tended to be discriminated against in the labor market. Because you only want the best for this employee, you are tempted to warn her not to make what you think would be a big mistake. **What should you do?**

A. Nothing. Her choices about her baby's name are none of your business.

B. Nothing right now, but leave a copy of the article somewhere she will run across it in hopes that she changes her mind.

C. Ask her whether she's sure that this name is a good idea, since it's so Black sounding.

D. Tell her about your concern, refer to the article, and tell her you only want the best for her and her family, but this isn't a good decision.

# Focused Issues Related to Protected Classes: National Origin

11.1 True or false: Citizenship and national origin are identical such that discrimination on the basis of citizenship is automatically discrimination on the basis of national origin.

11.2 True or false: Language may be the same thing as national origin because they are so closely linked. Thus, discrimination on the basis of language spoken may be disparate treatment on the basis of national origin.

11.3 If national origin is a kind of ethnic concept, is there such a thing as U.S. national origin? Why or why not?

11.4 Grocery Co. has a policy that says, "English is the official language of Grocery Co. Any employee who speaks a language other than English on Grocery Co. property will be disciplined." Dora is a native Spanish speaker, although she is fluent in English. One day, Dora spoke Spanish to a Spanish-speaking customer. Her supervisor overheard and suspended her without pay for a week. If Dora brings a national origin claim against Grocery Co. in an appropriate court, what is the likely result?

A. A loss for Dora because she was disciplined for conduct, not status.

B. A loss for Dora; since she did violate the policy, she cannot prove that the employer's reason is a pretext.

C. A win for Dora because the type of work she does at this type of workplace does not appear to necessitate speaking English at all times, so an English-only rule cannot be a BFOQ.

D. A win for Dora because disciplining her for speaking Spanish to a Spanish-speaking customer lacks good business sense.

**11.5** Luisa is Latina and works as a cashier at Andy's Foods, a local grocery store. She was born in the U.S. and is of Guatemalan descent. When she told her manager that she was pregnant and would need to take leave once the baby was born, her employer said, "This is the problem with you Mexicans. You're always having babies! Don't you know how birth control works? It's bad enough you come over here and steal jobs. You don't even do those jobs when you have them." Luisa left the office in tears, and the manager apologized, saying, "I'm sorry. I just kind of lost it because we're so short staffed. You're one of the good ones, and I never should have said those things." Two weeks later, though, she was terminated.

If Luisa, after exhausting her administrative remedies, brings an action against Andy's Foods, what is the likely result?

A. A win for Luisa because a rational factfinder could conclude that her national origin was a reason for her termination.

B. A win for Luisa because pregnant employees cannot be terminated unless the employer can demonstrate that being non-pregnant is a BFOQ.

C. A win for Andy's Foods because her national origin is not Mexican.

D. A win for Andy's Foods because Luisa was an at-will employee.

**11.6** Jie Li (in Chinese, Li Jie) is interviewing for a job with a local firm. Jie has excellent grades and significant relevant experience. He is a U.S. citizen, born of Chinese immigrant parents. During the interview, the interviewer asked Jie if he (the interviewer) could just call Jie, "Joe," because it's so much easier to pronounce. Jie said he would prefer not, that Jie was his name. The interviewer became a little defensive, but it seemed to Jie that the interview mostly proceeded fairly well. Jie was not hired, and instead a man named Brian Smith was. Jie called the interviewer and asked what he could have done better, and the interviewer assured him that he was well qualified, but just a bit more ethnic than he though the clientele would be comfortable with.

If Jie brings an action against the firm under Title VII, after exhausting any administrative remedies, what is the likely result?

A. A win for the firm because Jie is a U.S. citizen and thus not protected under Title VII's national origin clause.

B. A win for the firm because Jie was rude in the interview.

C. A win for Jie because a rational factfinder could conclude that the interviewer was not comfortable with Jie's Chinese-ness, as evidenced by asking to Anglicize his name and saying he was too "ethnic."

D. A win for Jie but only if the firm has some east Asian clients.

**11.7** Barker Farms hires many workers each summer to harvest its crops. David Smith, a Black man, and Felipe Ruiz, a Latino man, were born and grew up near the farm. They applied for jobs but were not hired. Instead, the farm relied on the H-2A visa program to hire temporary agricultural workers from other countries. The farm also hired some additional foreign born workers with green cards. A local paper did a feature on the business, highlighting its employment of foreign workers, and promoting that as a positive contribution to the community. The owner was quoted in the piece, praising the work ethic of foreign workers, and commenting that "folks born here just don't seem to have what it takes to put in a solid day of work anymore."

If the EEOC brings a claim against the farms on behalf of David and Felipe, what is the likely result?

A. A win for the EEOC because U.S. companies are required to prefer U.S. citizens for open positions.

B. A win for the EEOC because the employer appears to be using stereotypes about foreign-born workers in making its hiring decisions.

C. A win for Barker Farms because discriminating on the basis of citizenship does not violate Title VII.

D. A win for Barker Farms because there is no clear pattern of race or ethnic origin between who is hired and who is not.

**11.8** Serapia, Elena, Celia, and Maricela work in the harvesting unit for Fisheries, Inc. They are all Latinas. Several other women, Black, white, and Asian, work there as well, along with men of a variety of racial and ethnic groups. The supervisor of the harvesting unit is always saying something about Serapia, Elena, Celia, and Marcella. He calls them "hot tamales" and often makes explicit and graphic commentary about their body parts, asking whether they'd like a little bit of his "macho jalapeño." He also spreads rumors that they are very promiscuous, and spies on them as they attempt to use portable toilets. He does not do these things to the other women he supervises.

If the EEOC brings an action against Fisheries, Inc., what is the likely result?

A. A win for Fisheries, Inc. because not all women were subject to the harassment.

B. A win for Fisheries, Inc. unless the women reported the harassment internally.

C. A win for the EEOC because the supervisor engaged in quid pro quo harassment.

D. A win for the EEOC because the exclusive focus on Latinas and the graphic commentary with Spanish words along with stereotypes about promiscuity suggest that the supervisor is harassing these women because of their national origin.

Topic 12 Questions

# Focused Issues Related to Protected Classes: Sex

12.1 When the Supreme Court looked at the definition of race in 42 U.S.C. § 1981, and whether it protected white people as well as African Americans, it defined that term by looking to see what legislators said about race in the debates leading up to the bill's passage. Why is that strategy not available to courts wondering what conduct will be considered sex discrimination under Title VII?

12.2 You have probably heard about various gender gaps in the workplace. Women at just about all levels fall behind men in wages and level of professional achievement. In addition, the labor market is fairly sex segregated; women tend to be concentrated in about ten occupations, which have come to be called "pink collar" occupations like elementary education and nursing. What might be some reasons for these persistent gaps?

12.3 In *City of Los Angeles Department of Water & Power v. Manhart*, 435 U.S. 702 (1978), the employer required women to contribute more than men to the pension (defined benefit) plan. Was requiring greater pension contributions from women than men sex discrimination?

A. Yes; even though women as a group tend to live longer than men and so need more invested in advance of retirement to ensure enough funds to cover the longer time before they die, individual women won't necessarily live longer, and it is impossible to tell in advance which women will live longer and which will live shorter periods after retirement.

B. Yes; between salary and pension payments, women as a group would get less income from the employer.

C. No; between salary and pension payments, over the course of their lifetimes, women and men would get an equal amount of income.

D. No; life expectancy is a real difference between women and men as demonstrated by actuarial tables.

**12.4** Jane works at the reception desk of a mid-price hotel chain. She has very short hair, does not wear makeup, and wears slacks and button-down shirts to work. The hotel's dress code requires employees with customer contact to wear business casual dress. Slacks and button down shirts comply with this policy.

Jane's supervisor Rita thinks she has performed well and wants to promote Jane to Hospitality Manager. Rita's boss Evelyn approves the promotion. A week after this approval, Evelyn stops by the hotel where Jane works and sees her dressed as she normally is. Evelyn pulls Rita aside and tells her the promotion is off. The reason Evelyn gives is this: "We need our managers to reflect the image of our brand—cosmopolitan and polished. The softball coach, tomboy look is just not good enough."

If Jane sues for sex discrimination, what is the likely result?

A. Liability because the dress code discriminates on the basis of sex.

B. Liability because the manager engaged in sex stereotyping related to Jane's masculine appearance.

C. No liability because the manager was motivated by Jane's appearance, not because she was a woman.

D. No liability because the decision was made by a woman, and so cannot be sex discrimination.

**12.5** Blaine works in the kitchen at a restaurant as a sous chef. Carl and Dean, two other sous chefs, are always giving him a hard time. Every day, they call him names like "c***sucker" and "punk ass bitch." Carl and Dean have been physical a couple of times, too. Once Carl grabbed Blaine from behind around the chest and held him, while Dean grabbed his own crotch and said, "I'll bet you'd like a piece of this." Another time, Carl poked a broom handle into Blaine's buttocks and said, "look at that tight ass. Bet this makes you hot." Management knows all about this environment, but does nothing.

If Blaine sues for sexual harassment, will the restaurant likely be liable?

A. No because same sex harassment is not discrimination under Title VII.

B. No; this is just "horseplay" that Justice Scalia suggests won't violate Title VII.

C. Yes because Carl and Dean used words and engaged in conduct designed to threaten Blaine's masculinity as a way to humiliate him because he was male.

D. Yes, but only if Carl and Dean were gay.

**12.6** Josie was hired to work at the mine, one of only five women to be hired as a miner. Most of the work of the miners took place outdoors. There were no restroom facilities outdoors; the men simply walked some distance away when they had to urinate and did so in an out-of-the way spot. After Josie developed a urinary tract infection, she began taking unauthorized breaks to use the indoor restrooms. She was warned not to take those breaks, and when she continued to do so, she was terminated. No men took unauthorized breaks. If Josie brings an action challenging her termination as sex discrimination, what is her best claim?

A. Disparate treatment because only women lacked access to toilet facilities.

B. Disparate treatment because the lack of outdoor facilities meant that there "effectively" weren't any women's bathrooms.

C. Disparate impact because the effect of the lack of outdoor facilities was harder on women.

D. Disparate impact because the employer provided too few breaks.

**12.7** John is a substitute teacher in a public school system. After one day, the Principal tells him that he will not be called back because he is "too macho." Can John lose a disparate treatment case?

A. Yes, if nurturing and cooperation are skills required of teachers at this school.

B. Yes because men cannot bring sex stereotyping claims since stereotypes of men are all positive.

C. No because sex stereotyping automatically results in liability.

D. No as long as the decisionmaker was the opposite sex.

**12.8** Veronica's Closet is an upscale shop that sells women's lingerie. It caters to women, but markets substantially to straight men, who it hopes will either buy lingerie for female partners or encourage their female partners to buy lingerie there. The environment is designed to foster a tastefully sexy atmosphere. Sales clerks are required to wear name badges. The company has added something new to the name badges. In addition to their names, the badges will list some personal data. On men's, the badges list the man's height. Women's badges give their bra size. Artemis is so uncomfortable at having to wear something that refers to the size of her breasts that she is finding it harder and harder to concentrate at work.

If Artemis sues, seeking to remove the information about bra sizes from the name badges, what is her best argument in support of a discrimination claim?

A. Treating men and women differently in what information is printed on their name badges creates an undue burden on women.

B. Men and women can never be treated differently in workplace grooming codes.

C. Requiring this information on her name tag was conduct so severe—comparable to an assault—that it created an objectively hostile work environment.

D. The essence of the business is to sell clothing items and not to sell a sexualized experience.

**12.9** Oldfashioned Corp., which has 100 employees, has recently instituted a new maternity leave policy in an effort to appear more family friendly. The company has provided up to twelve weeks of unpaid leave for new parents who qualify under the Family and Medical Leave Act since that statute went into effect. The company has now added a pay component for mothers. Any women who give birth, adopt a child, or have a foster child placed in their care will be paid fifty percent of their salary for the period of leave they take. Darius is going to be a father soon. He plans to take six weeks of leave and has asked to be covered by the paid leave policy—that is, paid fifty percent of his salary. The President of the company does not want to comply with this request. The HR Director has come to you to ask whether the company has to. What advice should you give?

A. Give the leave, because pregnancy leave can't be treated more favorably than other types of leave.

B. Give the leave because providing a benefit for one sex that isn't available to the other likely violates Title VII.

C. Deny the leave because Darius is not pregnant, nor is fatherhood a medical condition connected to pregnancy within the meaning of the Pregnancy Discrimination Act.

D. Deny the leave because the policy does not favor all women, only mothers, and doesn't injure all men, only fathers. In the category of non-fathers, there are both women and men; so the classification is not sex discrimination.

**12.10** David works for Townsville's fire department. When his supervisor discovers that his birth certificate lists his sex as female, he is told that he must use the women's locker and restroom facilities. What is David's best argument that this violates Title VII.?

A. Being forced to use the locker and restroom facilities of a sex other than the one that David presents as currently affects a term, condition, or privilege of employment.

B. Treating David as if he was the sex assigned at birth is sex discrimination by definition.

C. Being forced to use the women's locker and restroom facilities creates an undue burden on David.

D. Maintaining sex segregated facilities is a per se violation of Title VII.

**12.11** Megan has worked for Craftsy, Inc. for five years. She was fired when her supervisor discovered she had married a woman. During the exchange at the time of the termination, the supervisor stated that she didn't discriminate; that she would have fired a man who married a man, as well. Megan brought a claim in an appropriate court, and Craftsy has moved to dismiss. What is the likely result?

A. Motion granted. This supervisor would treat both sexes the same, and equal opportunity "discrimination" doesn't violate Title VII.

B. Motion granted. Megan was terminated for conduct rather than status.

C. Motion denied. Craftsy's action infringed on the fundamental right to marry.

D. Motion denied. But for Megan's sex, her marriage to a woman would not have caused the termination.

**12.12** Boxco is a manufacturing facility that produces packaging materials for a variety of products. As you might expect, workers occasionally get injured on the job, and those workers are often accommodated by being assigned to light duty jobs. The rationale is that those workers would otherwise be receiving workers' comp and not working, so why not have them doing something to benefit the company to avoid drawing workers' comp. Nara is at a point in her pregnancy where her doctor has imposed restrictions on lifting heavy amounts. When Nara requests assignment to a light duty position, Boxco's HR director denies the request, saying that company policy limits light duty to those who suffer on-the job injuries. Nara is forced to take unpaid leave until after her baby is born.

If the EEOC brings a sex discrimination claim against Boxco for refusing to accommodate Nara's limitation, what is the likely result?

A. A win for Boxco unless some workers with off-the-job injuries have also been accommodated in the past.

B. A win for Boxco because pregnancy is a natural and desired state, not a disability.

C. A win for the EEOC because the Pregnancy Discrimination Act requires that pregnancy be accommodated when a doctor says that's necessary.

D. A win for the EEOC because the Pregnancy Discrimination Act requires leave for pregnancy if the employer provides leave for any other reason.

**12.13** Olivia worked for Lumen Corp. for several years before she started a family. She notified her employer that she would be taking a full 12 weeks of unpaid leave pursuant to the Family & Medical Leave Act after the birth of her baby. The company granted her leave. About three weeks before Olivia was due to return to work, she went on vacation with her spouse and new baby. Her supervisor saw her posts on Instagram and notified HR that Olivia was on vacation during her leave. The HR director contacted Olivia and told her that she had abused the leave and would be terminated as a result.

In an action under the FMLA, what is the likely result?

A. Liability for the employer because it invaded Olivia's privacy by acting based on a social media post.

B. Liability for the employer because a family vacation is not inconsistent with leave meant to allow a person to recover from birth (if necessary) and to bond with a new child.

C. No liability, because if you are well enough to go on vacation, you don't need FMLA leave.

D. No liability because employees who don't return to work as soon as they are physically able forfeit the protections of the FMLA.

**12.14** Paula works for a small business. She just had a baby who she is breastfeeding. When she told her supervisor that she would be returning to work, she asked for breaks and a clean space to express milk. Her supervisor said no, responding, "that is so gross. I think you really just need to be home with your baby. I'll make that easy for you. Don't come back."

Is this action likely to subject the employer to liability under any antidiscrimination law?

A. No, because lactation isn't an impairment, but instead a normal bodily function, and so doesn't need to be accommodated under the ADA.

B. No, because lactation isn't a dysfunction caused by pregnancy or childbirth, but instead a normal bodily function, and so not protected by the PDA.

C. Yes, because lactation is related to pregnancy and childbirth, and discharging someone for lactating is thus sex discrimination.

D. Yes, because all employers are required to provide breaks and a clean space to express milk.

**12.15** Pete worked for about a decade at a large accounting firm after college, but he has been a stay-at-home dad since the birth of his child five years ago. Now that his child is entering kindergarten, Pete is looking to reenter the workforce. At an interview with Pence Waterless, a large accounting firm, the interviewer asked about the gap in Pete's resume. Pete explained that he'd been the primary caregiver for his child. When he revealed that information, the interviewer looked surprised and said, "Really, dude? Well, I guess that's a choice. I mean if you *like* kids or can't do other things." A week later, Pete was told that the firm hired a different man, one straight out of college.

If Pete brings a Title VII sex discrimination claim against Pence Waterless, assuming he exhausts his administrative remedies first, is he likely to get past a motion to dismiss?

A. No, because Pete's comparator is also a man.

B. No, because men aren't protected by Title VII.

C. Yes, because Pete was clearly more qualified than the man straight out of college.

D. Yes, because the interviewer seemed to react negatively to Pete's choice to be a caregiver, repeating stereotypes about real men not being suited for that role.

**12.16** Quinta is pregnant and having terrible morning sickness. It is making her late to work, and her employer has a policy that any employee late to work more than 4 times in a six-month period will be terminated. Quinta explained to her supervisor why she was late, but her supervisor was not particularly sympathetic. The fourth time that she was late, her supervisor told her that if she was late one more time, she would be fired. Quinta tried very hard to be on time, but the next week, she was 2 minutes late. She'd had to pull over in traffic to vomit and got stuck in a traffic jam. She was fired.

If Quinta brings a disparate treatment action in an appropriate court after exhausting her administrative remedies, is she likely to prevail?

A. No; employer work rules can only be challenged if they are facially discriminatory, and this rule applied to all employees equally.

B. No; the pregnancy discrimination act does not require an employer to make exceptions to neutral work rules for pregnant employees.

C. Yes; morning sickness is a medical condition related to pregnancy and so must be accommodated.

D. Yes; but-for her pregnancy, Quinta wouldn't have been terminated.

**12.17** The Supreme Court's decision in *Bostock v. Clayton County*, 140 S. Ct. 1731 (2020), was hailed as a great victory in a lot of ways for the LGBT+ community. Recall that the Court held in that case that discrimination on the basis of sexual orientation or gender identity was sex discrimination under Title VII as a matter of logic and the plain text of the statute. In explaining its reasoning, the Court gave several examples of why this was true. For example, if an employer would not fire a woman because she was dating a man, but would fire a man for the same conduct, dating a man, that employer was clearly making a distinction between those employees based on their sex. Similarly, if it would fire a person who wore a skirt to work when their sex assigned at birth was male but wouldn't fire an employee whose sex assigned at birth was female, it was making a distinction based on the employee's sex.

Some commentators have raised concerns that the Court's reasoning may not reach all members of the LGBT+ community. One particular concern focuses on protections of bisexual people. Do you think that discrimination on the basis of bisexuality violates Title VII after *Bostock*? Why or why not?

# Focused Issues Related to Protected Classes: Religion

13.1 Alvin is Afro-Caribbean-American. He grew up in the U.S., but his parents are from Jamaica, and his distant ancestors from Africa. Alvin is a follower of the Rastafari movement and believes that the Bible forbids him from cutting his hair or shaving his beard. He has applied to work as a salesperson at Bland, a large, national clothing store that celebrates, "All-American" youth culture. The company's personal appearance policy requires employees who grow visible facial hair to be clean shaven. Customer surveys done every couple of years consistently show that customers associate a lack of facial hair with youth. On average, about 3% of customers say they would stop shopping at any Bland that had a salesperson with visible facial hair. Alvin explained his religious views and asked the employer to waive the policy as to him. Bland refused to waive the policy and told Alvin that it would hire him if he would shave.

If Alvin, after pursuing the appropriate administrative process, sues Bland for discrimination based on his religion, what is the likely outcome?

A. A win for Bland, as long as the risk of losing customers is more than a de minimis undue hardship.

B. A win for Bland because Alvin's religion isn't a bona fide religion.

C. A win for Alvin because customer preference can never be a BFOQ.

D. A win for Alvin because he sincerely believes he cannot shave.

13.2 Mom & Pop Groceries is a small store that employs 20 people. It is owned by Joe and Mary, who are Seventh Day Adventists. Seventh Day Adventists are Christians who observe the Sabbath on Saturdays. Accordingly, the store is closed on Saturday but open on Sunday. Joe and Mary require every employee to work Sundays on a rotating schedule, so that everyone works about two Sundays a month. Joe and Mary hire Andrew to be a new cashier. Andrew is a devout Christian who believes it is a sin to work on Sundays. When he is first scheduled for a Sunday, he tells Joe and Mary that he cannot work on any Sunday for religious reasons. Joe and Mary fire him.

If Andrew sues Joe and Mary under Title VII, what is the likely result?

A. Andrew will likely lose because Joe, Mary, and he are all Christians, so religion can't be the reason for his discharge.

B. Andrew will likely lose because accommodating him would discriminate against all of the other employees on the basis of religion.

C. Andrew will likely lose because Joe and Mary as religious employers can't be sued consistent with the First Amendment; they have an automatic ministerial exception.

D. Andrew will likely lose because accommodating his religious practice would pose an undue hardship on Joe and Mary, since they run a small business that presumably needs everyone to work, and exempting one employee would burden the others.

**13.3** Temple Beth-el is a Jewish synagogue that runs a daycare, which is open to members of the community, regardless of their religion. It only hires Jewish employees for the daycare. Is this likely a violation of Title VII?

A. No, because daycare workers are, by definition, ministerial employees, and courts cannot interfere with those employment decisions.

B. No, because religious organizations can discriminate on the basis of religion in hiring for any kind of position carrying out the organization's work.

C. Yes, because the daycare is open to anyone regardless of religion, so the synagogue can't discriminate in the operation of the daycare.

D. Yes, because the essence of a daycare worker's job is to engage in caregiving tasks, not religious indoctrination.

**13.4** Craftsy, Inc. is a for-profit, closely held corporation. Its owners have imbued the company's culture with their religious views. Under current law, can it claim the exemptions provided for religious corporations? Why or why not?

**13.5** St. Benedict's is a Catholic high school. Like many high schools, it has a fairly robust set of extracurricular activities to support the spiritual, physical, and emotional growth of its students, which the school sees as intertwined. This includes sports teams for students to participate in and compete against other schools in the area. One of those sports is soccer. Alex, a white man, is the boys soccer coach, and he is well liked by the kids, parents, teachers, and administrators. The soccer team is one of the best in the region. One day, Alex seemed especially happy, and the kids asked why. He shared that he had eloped over the weekend and married the love of his life, a Black woman. When the administration found out that Alex was in an interracial marriage, it terminated him.

Alex exhausted his administrative remedies and brought an action under Title VII for race discrimination. St. Benedict's has filed a motion for summary judgment on the ground that the ministerial exception bars the suit against them. Is there any possibility that this could be granted?

A. No; soccer is a secular activity, and that is bolstered by the fact that competition doesn't seem to be limited to other Catholic schools.

B. No; the ministerial exception only allows religious organizations to discriminate on the basis of religion, and this is discrimination on the basis of race.

C. Yes; Catholic schools are automatically granted ministerial exceptions for violations of Title VII.

D. Yes; it is possible, given the way the school views spirituality as intertwined with other aspects of its extracurricular activities, that the schools' coaches might qualify as ministerial employees under that fact-intensive test.

**13.6** Imagine instead that Alex's spouse is a man, and St. Benedict's has not invoked the ministerial exception as a defense. Instead, it has argued that the Church does not recognize same sex marriages. Is Alex likely to prevail in a Title VII sex discrimination claim?

A. Probably; without the ministerial exception, the school is just like any other employer.

B. Probably; but-for Alex's sex, his marriage to a man would likely not be a problem.

C. Probably not; even though Alex has styled this as a sex discrimination claim, the school is allowed to discriminate on the basis of religion under Title VII, and so can penalize Alex for not following Church doctrine.

D. Probably not; the religious organization exemption provides that Churches are allowed to discriminate under Title VII.

# Focused Issues Related to Protected Classes: Age

**14.1** Facebook allows people to place ads that target people based on a variety of characteristics including age. Some of these ads are from employers, including Facebook itself. Facebook placed one of those ads, targeting users between 18 and 54. Does this action violate the ADEA?

A. Probably not, because some people in the protected class (ages 40-54) will see the ad.

B. Probably not, because age is just one factor used to target users.

C. Probably, if Facebook intends this targeting to yield an applicant pool of mostly young people.

D. Probably, because targeting age this way is not reasonable.

**14.2** Imagine that instead of targeting ages, Facebook instead targets people with an affinity for the music of the 1960s to be excluded from any ads. Assume that this would remove a disproportionate number of people over 40 years of age. The job in question is for a content moderator–someone who will resolve whether posts ought to be removed when reported. If a 50-year-old in Missouri brings a disparate impact lawsuit under the ADEA, is that person likely to win?

A. Probably, because even though musical taste is a factor other than age, it seems arbitrary and not reasonable given what the position is and the usual kinds of factors employers consider in hiring

B. Probably, because understanding current popular music is probably a bona fide occupational qualification for a content moderator.

C. Probably not because Facebook isn't singling out age any more.

D. OK Boomer.

**14.3** Why might the outcome be different if the lawsuit just described was brought in Illinois?

**14.4** Blooble is a tech company started by college students a few years ago, and it has enjoyed rapid success. The founders, Lars and Sven, who recently graduated, devised a way of organizing large amounts of digital information to make retrieval much easier. In order to secure financing, Lars and Sven brought in older, more established business folks as managers, and now that the company has several hundred employees, those managers are still at the top of the organization and making the most money. Although these managers are older, none seems anxious to retire; they're mostly in their forties and fifties and enjoy the work and the very large income. Lars and Sven want to get rid of these people, though, because Lars and Sven believe that they are too old to keep up with the changes. They devise a new company policy: mandatory retirement for anyone who has been out of college or graduate school for longer than fifteen years. Larry and Sven state publicly that the new policy is a way to ensure that its workforce is up to date on relevant knowledge and skills. Can a person subject to this mandatory retirement policy state a claim for age discrimination?

A. No, because the policy doesn't explicitly differentiate based on age, and although time out of school may be somewhat correlated with age, that correlation isn't perfect: a person can graduate from college or graduate school at any age.

B. No, because employers are allowed to consider salary costs in making business decisions.

C. Yes, because the policy was adopted with the purpose that older workers be discharged.

D. Yes, because Blooble would have to prove that education is more linked to success than is experience.

**14.5** The Supreme Court has noted that the age discrimination is significantly different from discrimination on the basis of the classes protected by Title VII. In what way has the Court suggested that age discrimination might be less illegitimate than discrimination prohibited by Title VII?

**14.6** One of Congress's findings made in the ADEA referred to the harm that negative stereotypes of older workers played in employer discrimination. Not all stereotypes of older workers are necessarily negative, however. Thus, some courts have found that employer decisions motivated by the effects of assumptions that are not negative, like that older workers are more likely to have larger savings for retirement, do not violate the ADEA. Do you think this is an error that the Supreme Court or Congress should fix? Why or why not?

# Focused Issues Related to Protected Classes: Disability

**15.1** True or false: Jill has a seizure disorder that comes and goes. She'll be fine, and then, unpredictably, she'll have a seizure. For the last sixth months, she's taken medication that has prevented any seizures. Thus, Jill is not disabled within the meaning of the statute.

**15.2** True or false: The answer for Jill might have been different in 2007.

**15.3** True or false: The ADA has some limitations that are quite different from the Title VII model. For example, employers are explicitly limited in the kinds of things they can ask an applicant if those things might be considered a medical examination.

**15.4** What is an employer's duty toward a current employee who develops a disability that impairs their ability to do the job?

A. The employer must retain the person in the job or move the person to a new job.

B. The employer has no duty at all toward the person and can fire the person if the person can't do the job as well as before.

C. The employer must accommodate the employee's disability if the employee is able to do the essential functions of the job that way and the accommodation poses no undue hardship on the employer.

D. The employer can terminate the employee if the employer provides disability insurance to provide the employee with income while the employee is unable to work.

**15.5** Zed is an alcoholic, who, as a result of his physical or mental addiction to alcohol, drinks too much, frequently oversleeps and gets to work late. Can his employer terminate him for being tardy?

A. Yes, but only if working at specific times is an essential function of his job.

B. No, unless the employer has given notice of a zero-tolerance policy.

C. No, if a mental health professional characterizes the alcoholism as a disability.

D. Yes, because an employer need not accommodate the consequences of an employee's use of alcohol even if a mental health professional would categorize the alcoholism as a disability.

**15.6** Edward has applied to work as a forklift driver at Safeco. He has mild narcolepsy. Narcolepsy causes people to fall asleep for short periods of time. The person can't control or predict when these episodes will occur, although they often occur in response to a stressful event. The drugs Edward takes are entirely effective, and Edward has had no episodes of involuntary loss of consciousness since he started using them.

Safeco's HR director tells Edward that it is too risky to hire him. Assuming the ADA as amended applies, if Edward sues Safeco, is he likely to be successful?

A. No, because Edward's narcolepsy makes him a direct threat to the safety of others.

B. No, because the medication so fully compensates for Edward's impairment that he is not disabled.

C. Yes, because the HR director regarded Edward as disabled.

D. Yes, because the HR director had a duty to accommodate Edward's narcolepsy.

**15.7** Stan Smith was a news anchor on a local station. In 2019, he suffered a stroke on the air. The episode was quite disturbing to viewers, who saw him lose consciousness and fall off of his chair. They also saw his coworkers panicking to get him medical attention. Fortunately for Stan, he has now completely recovered. He has no visible effects of the stroke. The station has welcomed him back to work, but not as an anchor. Instead, it has given him a research job, which pays less. He is also kept off camera. The station has not been able to find a permanent anchor to replace him, and Stan would like his old job back. The station has refused, saying that despite his great qualifications, viewers would not accept Stan as an anchor and would be afraid that they would see him have another stroke.

Stan has sued the station under the Americans with Disabilities Act, seeking reinstatement. The station has moved to dismiss. What is the likely result?

A. The motion will be granted because Stan is only being regarded as disabled, and so his preference is not entitled to an accommodation.

B. The motion will be denied because regardless of whether the station is regarding Stan as disabled or as having a record of a disability, it is only because of his stroke that the station won't allow him to be an anchor again.

C. The motion will be denied because Stan has an actual disability that must be accommodated.

D. The motion will be granted because Stan is not disabled within the meaning of the ADA because he has completely recovered.

For questions 15.8–15.9, consider the following facts

Claude has a condition known as "pseudofolliculitis barbae," which describes persistent irritation and ingrown hairs caused by shaving. Inflamed papules can develop, and over time, they can cause keloid scarring. Doctors recommend that men with this condition not shave, or at least not shave closely.

He has applied to work as a salesperson at Bland, a large, national clothing store that celebrates "All-American" youth culture. The company's personal appearance policy requires employees who have visible facial hair to be clean shaven. Customer surveys done every couple of years consistently show that customers associate a lack of facial hair with youth. On average, about 3% of customers say they would stop shopping at any Bland that had a salesperson with visible facial hair. Bland does not hire him, but says it would if he would shave.

**15.8** If Claude, after pursuing the appropriate administrative process, sues Bland for disability discrimination under the ADA as amended, and Bland wins, what is the most likely reason?

A. Claude is not an individual with a disability under the ADA if he does not currently have the inflammation and papules that are caused by PFB.

B. Claude is not a qualified individual because he cannot perform the essential functions of the job.

C. Claude is not entitled to an accommodation because shaving is not a major life activity.

D. Bland does not need to accommodate Claude as long as it could demonstrate that doing so would injure its customer relations and cause it real financial loss.

**15.9** If Claude, after pursuing the appropriate administrative process, sues Bland for disability discrimination under the ADA as amended, and Claude wins, what is the most likely reason?

A. The tiny risk of lower sales may be more than a de minimis hardship, but it is not enough to make allowing a few exceptions to this part of the grooming code an unreasonable accommodation.

B. Bland was motivated by stereotypes about youth culture in setting its grooming policy.

C. The grooming code imposes an undue hardship on Claude.

D. The grooming code is facially discriminatory.

**15.10** Amy worked in the stockroom at Superstore, Inc., earning $13.00 per hour. She suffered a permanent injury on the job to her back, and her injury meant she could no longer lift anything heavier than 20 pounds. Superstore had an opening in the deli, where Amy would earn the same hourly wage. Amy was qualified for that position—it was an entry-level position—but instead of automatically transferring Amy there, Superstore considered her along with other applicants for that position. Superstore ultimately hired someone more qualified—the person hired had 5 years' experience working at a grocery store deli at another chain store. Superstore instead placed Amy in a janitorial position at another store, where her hourly wage is $7 per hour.

If, after exhausting her administrative remedies, Amy files an action under the ADA and wins, what is the most likely reason?

A. By looking to relative qualifications, Superstore regarded Amy as disabled and engaged in disparate treatment.

B. Transfer to a vacant position is a reasonable accommodation, and Superstore should have allowed Amy to transfer to a vacant position without competing against other applicants.

C. The ADA requires that Superstore maintain Amy's salary regardless of how her disability is accommodated.

D. Because Amy was a current employee, her qualifications for any other position are irrelevant.

**15.11** Imagine instead that Amy didn't seek to transfer to a different position, but instead had asked to be provided a small robot that worked like a mini forklift and which could do any lifting over 20 pounds that had to be done. Would Superstore have to provide that? Why or why not?

**15.12** Grocery, Inc. has had some disruptive employees in the past. In order to foster a more harmonious working environment, it now uses a personality test based on the Myers-Briggs personality inventory. That test has questions that can sometimes lead to answers that indicate cognitive, emotional, or behavioral disorders. Grocery administers the test as part of the online application process and decides who to interview based on their performance on the test. If use of the test is challenged in an appropriate case, what is the likely result?

A. No liability for Grocery because the test is narrowly tailored to detect employees who will be the best fit.

B. No liability for Grocery because applicants consent to the test by applying.

C. Liability for Grocery because at least some questions on the test likely constitute a medical inquiry, which cannot be made pre-offer.

D. Liability for Grocery because the test does not focus on knowledge required for the job, and thus the test is not job related.

**15.13** Kevin worked as a lineman for the Electric Company. As part of his job, Kevin sometimes has to climb poles, and sometimes be raised to great heights in a crane or a "cherry picker," which is a sort of bucket-like platform on an extendable crane arm, to reach the heights that lines would be strung. This isn't an everyday task, but it is something that linemen do fairly frequently. After a COVID-19 infection, Kevin developed persistent vertigo, a condition that leaves him unsteady at heights sometimes. Kevin's doctor has suggested that this condition could last the rest of Kevin's life. Kevin has sought an accommodation, asking that he not be assigned to tasks that require him to work at heights.

Does the Electric Company have to provide this accommodation?

A. No; as long as working at heights is an essential element of the job of lineman, which the facts suggest is true.

B. No; working at heights is not a major life activity since most people don't do it.

C. Yes; Kevin's impairment is the only thing keeping him from performing the essential functions of his job.

D. Yes; this accommodation will protect Kevin and his coworkers from the direct threat posed by Kevin's impairment.

**15.14** Loren works for Penderby Energy Co. as a manager. Last year, Loren's child was diagnosed with a rare childhood cancer. Treatment has been an expensive drain on the company's plan. Loren's manager is also concerned that Loren has been a bit distracted by worry. Loren's work has not suffered yet, but the manager is worried just the same. The company is going to impose a Reduction in Force (RIF) because of declining profits, and Loren's manager recommends Loren be one of the employees laid off based on these concerns. Should the company be worried about liability under the ADA?

A. Yes, because the ADA requires that Loren's job be protected at least until the child is in remission.

B. Yes, because terminating someone because they are associated with a person with a disability, whether because of the expense of that disability or fears of distraction, violates the ADA.

C. No, because the ADA does not apply to company-wide RIFs.

D. No, because Loren doesn't have a disability, isn't regarded as having a disability, and doesn't have a record of a disability.

**15.15** Mark is a lawyer who works for the civil appeals division of the state Attorney General's office. Most of his work is researching and writing briefs, with the occasional oral argument. The briefing schedule is very predictable and stable. Mark has Crohn's disease, which is an inflammatory bowel disease that can cause abdominal pain, severe diarrhea, fatigue, weight loss and malnutrition. When his condition is under control, Mark can function just as well as any person without the disease, but when he has a flare-up, Mark needs to be close to a bathroom, able to lie down when necessary, and able to strictly control his intake of food and water. It is much easier to manage a flare-up at home than in the office.

The office has a policy that requires lawyers and support staff to be physically at the office from 9 am to 5 pm unless they are in court. There was a brief time in 2020, when courts were mostly shut down, that the office allowed those who could to work from home.

But everyone has been required to be in person since late 2020. Based on his condition, Mark has asked to be able to work from home on days he is having a flare-up. His office denied the accommodation, and Mark had to resign once he exhausted his sick time, as a result. It was too hard to go to the office when he had a flare-up.

If Mark brings an action against the Attorney General for prospective, injunctive relief under the ADA for failure to accommodate his disability, and loses, what is the most likely reason?

A. Mark does not have a disability unless he is in a flare-up that will last for more than 6 months.

B. Mark's request will create a greater-than-de-minimis burden on the AG's office.

C. Working at the office is an essential function of Mark's job.

D. The AG is exempt from complying with the ADA under the Eleventh Amendment.

**15.16** If Mark brings an action against the Attorney General for prospective, injunctive relief under the ADA for failure to accommodate his disability, and *wins*, what is the most likely reason?

A. The AG's policy is a per se violation of the ADA.

B. The AG's policy is a direct threat to public health because it doesn't have a COVID exception.

C. The AG's office is estopped from limiting work from home options based on its conduct during the quarantine period.

D. The requirement that lawyers work at the office is not an essential function of the job.

**15.17** Nell recently passed the bar and is interviewing for jobs with local firms. She had a great first interview at Littlethorpe Jenkins for an associate position. The interview took place over Zoom, and the team was very impressed with Nell's credentials, grades, writing sample, and her responses to their questions. She seemed bright and personable. When the firm invited Nell for a callback, things did not go as well. Nell arrived at the office with her service animal and her long white cane. Nell's vision is severely impaired, and she relies on the cane and service animal to navigate obstacles. She also relies on assistive technologies to research, write, and engage in other lawyering tasks.

Out of courtesy, the firm completed the interview, but it did not offer Nell a position. The hiring partner informed her that the reason the firm didn't hire her was that the firm's work was too sensitive and high-stakes for someone unable to see. They were concerned that Nell would never be able to function at a high enough level to meet the demands of their particular practice.

If, after exhausting her administrative remedies, Nell files an action against the firm, what is the likely result?

A. A win for Nell because the firm didn't even engage in the interactive process with her.

B. A win for Nell but only if she is willing to provide her own assistive measures to enable her to do the work.

C. A win for the firm because the demands of their particular practice made accommodation impossible.

D. A win for the firm because the accommodations Nell would require would impose an undue burden on it.

**15.18** The Americans with Disabilities Act is similar to Title VII and the Age Discrimination in Employment Act, in that it prohibits disparate treatment and disparate impact, both. Unlike Title VII and the ADEA, disparate impact cases are almost never brought under the ADA, though.

Some commentators have suggested that the reason for this is that the accommodations requirement serves a similar purpose and provides a more convenient vehicle. Others have pointed to the diversity of those in the disability community, and even more broadly, in the group of people protected by the ADA. What do you think the reason is, and why? Is it one of these, a combination of both, or something else? Explain your reasoning in your answer.

# Sample Exam Questions

1. Ghost in the Machine (GitM) is a large tech company that develops artificial intelligence software for businesses. One of GitM's main new products in development involves facial recognition technology that will be used to detect emotional states.

   GitM has more than 500 employees in offices across the country. Its headquarters are in St. Louis. Like many tech companies, GitM is not the most diverse. Only 4% of workers are Black and 6% are Latino—1% are Black women, and 2% are Latina. The rest of the workers are fairly evenly split between Asian and Anglo workers, although men outnumber women by about two to one.

   Within its research division are two research scientists who created and lead a team focused on ethical AI. One of those scientists, Alexa Adan, is a Black woman, and the other, Bell Blake is an Anglo woman. Alexa created an affinity group for Black engineers and researchers at the company, and both women are active members of the affinity group for female engineers and researchers. Both women also regularly publish research with co-authors outside of GitM, and while GitM must review the research before it is published, that review process generally goes smoothly and quickly. The only time changes have been requested in the past, it has been to ensure no sensitive information about GitM is inadvertently shared.

   With the growth of facial recognition software, Alexa began to investigate racial bias in that software. As part of her work, she co-authored a study highlighting the frequency of bias in facial analysis programs. That study showed disparate error rates of the facial analysis system at issue. The error rate for light-skinned people was .8% but for dark skinned people was 35%. Alexa submitted the study internally for review, and a few days later, submitted an abstract describing the study in general terms, to a conference for presentation.

   About a week after the conference submission, GitM's head of AI, Steve Smith, called Alexa and demanded that she withdraw the conference submission. When Alexa asked why, Smith said that the paper was not up to the quality of a peer review publication and that Alexa was engaged in "advocacy disguised as science." When Alexa asked Smith whether he would have taken the same action if Bell had submitted the paper, Smith exploded: "That's the trouble with you, Alexa. You're obsessed with being a victim, creating a toxic environment at GitM, always focused on race, after we gave you a chance no other tech company would have. How many Black women have the budget and profile you do because of your position here? It's not brilliance that's getting you those conference invitations." Smith continued, "and how stupid do you have to be to undermine the whole premise of our biggest new product?" Smith called security to escort Alexa out of the building and locked her out of company files. He had the personal things in her office packed and shipped to her home along with a letter formally terminating her.

Bell was horrified by Alexa's firing. She became openly critical of Smith, tweeting her concerns about Alexa's firing and other issues she saw as undermining the ethics in AI work within GitM and diversity efforts within the company: "Say you have a problem with consistently alienating Black women and have caused serious damage in their lives. You could: A) try to undo that damage B) try to find more Black people to like you (the tokenism approach). Good luck ...."

She also wrote an automated script to look through her emails to gather evidence of discrimination against Alexa. About a month later, GitM cut off Bell's email access and began investigating her activity. One week after that, Bell was terminated. In a public statement about the termination, GitM said, "After conducting a review of this manager's conduct, we confirmed that there were multiple violations of our code of conduct, as well as of our security policies, which included the exfiltration of confidential business-sensitive documents and private data of other employees."

When GitM announced it was firing Bell, it also announced it was making changes into its research and diversity policies. Smith, in an internal email, apologized to staff for how Alexa's departure was handled: "I heard and acknowledge what Dr. Adan's exit signified to female technologists, to those in the Black community and other underrepresented groups who are pursuing careers in tech, and to many who care deeply about GitM's responsible use of AI. It led some to question their place here, which I regret." The ethical AI team was reorganized, and Robert Cole, a Black man and vice president in the engineering department, was named to lead a new center of expertise "on responsible AI within GitM research."

Analyze any claims Alexa and Bell might have against GitM. What defense strategies or defenses might GitM use? Be sure to analyze the relevant facts and explain which party likely has the stronger position and why.

2. Over the course of the semester, a few cases and hypotheticals involved situations where rights within Title VII seemed in conflict. Several of those were in the religion context. For example, one person's religious practice may require them to evangelize, which involves recruiting others to one's faith, or simply "witnessing" about one's beliefs or experiences in faith. That practice might interfere with another person's right to practice their religion without interference or their right to be free from religion. Even more broadly, an employer's rights to practice religion might interfere with rights against sex or race discrimination, for example.

   How should these kinds of conflicts—especially conflicts between religion and some other protected status, like sex or race—be handled by courts and why?

**3.** A few years ago, a casting call for the off-Broadway production of *Hamilton* set off a wave of controversy. As you may know, the hip-hop musical is about Alexander Hamilton, and the roles are deliberately multi-racial. The call specified that the company was recruiting performers who were "non-white men and women." That call was criticized as violating equal opportunity policies, to which the show's producer responded:

> The producers of *Hamilton* regret the confusion that's arisen from the recent posting of an open call casting notice for the show. It is essential to the storytelling of *Hamilton* that the principal roles—which were written for non-white characters (excepting King George)—be performed by non-white actors. This adheres to the accepted practice that certain characteristics in certain roles constitute a "bona fide occupational qualification" that is legal. This also follows in the tradition of many shows that call for race, ethnicity, or age specific casting, whether it's *The Color Purple* or *Porgy & Bess* or *Matilda*. The casting call will be amended to also include language we neglected to add, that is, we welcome people of all ethnicities to audition for *Hamilton*.

What are the legal and policy arguments against the kind of casting call the producers put out? What legal and policy arguments support it? Which side do you think is stronger and why?

# Additional Issue Spotter Questions

1. Amina Okoro, immigrated to the United States from Nigeria ten years ago. She works for Younkers, a department store, in St. Louis County. Okoro, a practicing Muslim, has worked for about four years in the women's clothing department and has excellent performance reviews. Late last year, Okoro got engaged to be married. She told her supervisor, Mary Smith, that she was going to begin to wear a traditional Muslim head covering (a khimar or hijab) at work because getting married made her feel closer to her faith and wearing a head covering was a required expression of that faith. Citing Younkers' dress code, which prohibits "hats, caps, visors, bandanas, head coverings, etc.," Smith told Okoro she could not wear the head covering at work. The dress code also provides this:

> A professional image is projected in each employee's individual appearance. All employees should strive to present a well-groomed and professional appearance appropriate for a first-class department store. In maintaining this policy, supervisors will enforce the policy in letter and spirit. Employee grooming, dress and fashions should be professional, of moderate style, and within the standards generally observed in the business community. Jeans are not acceptable. Extremes should be avoided.

Following this general description, the policy listed clothing that was prohibited, including athletic shoes, shorts, clothes that were too tight, very short skirts, and shirts or dresses with spaghetti straps. The head covering ban was on that list.

After Okoro's request was denied, she filed a charge of religious discrimination with the Equal Employment Opportunity Commission and the Missouri Commission on Human Rights. When Younkers received notice of the charge, the Human Resources director interviewed Mary Smith to gather facts for the agency investigation. Smith stated that she was just following the policy and she worried that customers would be put off by an employee who wore a traditional Muslim head covering, which might hurt sales. The Younkers store is in a part of the county where 87% of the population identify as Christian. About 10% of people who live in the city of St. Louis, though, are Muslim. About 43% of Muslim women in the region wear head coverings. No measurable percentage of women of any other religion in the region wear head coverings.

Okoro did not wear the head covering to work, waiting for the legal process to provide a remedy. About two weeks after Smith was interviewed, Okoro was working on the sales floor when her mother stopped by to ask a question. Okoro greeted her mother in Igbo, the language the family speaks at home. Smith heard and later that day, sharply reprimanded Okoro for speaking a language other than English. Every day for the next three weeks, when Okoro would speak to Smith, Smith would snap, "speak English!" She also often added something like this: "I won't have that oogity boogity nonsense when customers can hear! It's bad enough you want to look like some terrorist sympathizer. Leave the jungle at home." Okoro always spoke to Smith in English and in fact speaks fluent English—English is the official language of Nigeria—but she has an accent. Upset by Smith's behavior, Okoro decided to begin wearing her headscarf.

The first time that Okoro reported to work wearing the headscarf, Smith told her to remove it. When she refused to remove it, she was sent home, pursuant to Younkers' policy. She wore the headscarf each of the next two workdays and was ultimately disciplined for insubordination and terminated.

Okoro plans to continue to pursue her legal remedies. What federal claims might she have and how will she prove them? What defenses will Younkers raise? Who is more likely to be successful and why?

**2.** On the Third Day (OTD) is a discount home goods outlet that sells off-price and closeout home goods. It operates 300 stores across the country, and it is a closely held corporation, run by a small group of family members who are conservative Christians. They view their business as a home beautification ministry, "Bringing the beauty of the Lord into people's homes by making their homes beautiful as affordably as possible." OTD has a dress code for its employees:

> Employees should dress modestly, with decency and propriety. Tight or revealing clothing is not permitted. Men must wear khaki or dark-colored twill slacks. Women may wear similar slacks or loose-fitting skirts that fall no higher than just below the knee. Men should wear collared button-down or short-sleeve polo shirts. Women should wear blouses that button up or that are crew-necked or collared. V-necks are not permitted. Shirts for women must have at least 3/4 length sleeves.
>
> Men must be clean shaven with no piercings or tattoos. Their hair must be no longer than to their collar and may not be dyed. No jewelry other than a wedding ring is permitted.
>
> Women may wear simple jewelry and have a single piercing in each ear, but they may not have tattoos. Hair should be at least mid-length, falling below the collar, but may be worn back or up in simple styles. Hair may be dyed, but not with extreme colors.

Rhonda James is African-American. She has naturally coarse and tightly curly hair that grows naturally into an Afro style. She has, at times, straightened her hair using chemical processes or a flat iron. She also has sometimes kept her hair short and worn hair pieces (artificial hair) with straight hair. Her hair is naturally a very light brown color. Rhonda has worked for OTD for five years and has always received good performance reviews and raises.

Rhonda decided that she was tired of the expense and damage that straightening does to her hair and so stopped straightening it. She also was tired of the pain and expense of using hair pieces. They often pulled at her hair or squeezed her scalp uncomfortably. Thus, Rhonda decided while on vacation to stop straightening her hair and to wear it in a natural style. In its natural style, Rhonda's hair will not easily grow below her collar, but instead mostly grows out from her head. It is currently about two inches long, all over her head. To help Rhonda get used to her new hairstyle, Rhonda's hair stylist put in some blonde highlights in strands that frame her face.

Rhonda returned from vacation with her new hairstyle, and she was called into the store manager's office. The manager, Tim Remo, asked her about her "unfeminine" and "extreme" hair style choice. It was too short, too curly, and the blond highlights, he claimed, were "unnatural." He warned her that her hair violated the company's dress code and sent her home. Rhonda could come back, Remo said, when her hair was returned to its previous style. He did not care how Rhonda accomplished that—by straightening her hair and dying it a darker brown or wearing hair pieces—but she couldn't keep her current style and her job. When Rhonda warned Remo that she though his actions were discriminatory, he responded that the company's policy followed a higher law and that no law could infringe on the owners' religious beliefs.

Evaluate any claims Rhonda may have under Title VII, doing a full legal analysis of those potential claims, and commenting on their strength or weakness. As part of that analysis, identify the arguments OTD will make, analyze them, and also evaluate their strength or weakness.

**3.** John Higgins is a 32-year-old African American man. He went to an elite high school and started working in the City Brewery's main bottleworks. The positions he held at the brewery were each a progressive step in his career. He started working at the plant as a warehouse utility worker. Next, he worked as a packaging operator, and then he became a line supervisor. On September 1, he applied to become a packaging shift manager.

When Higgins sought a shift manager job, the brewery hierarchy was like this from top to bottom for each separate bottling facility on the production line (outside of each bottling facility was the executive team including the Chief Operating Officer and the other executive managers for non-production departments, and inside each facility were other workers and supervisors for things like maintenance): one brewery manager, two shift managers, six line supervisors, and then a number of lead persons, operators, and hourly workers. The City Brewery's main bottleworks has never had a Black brewery manager or shift manager, but five of the six line supervisors there are Black.

In April of the same year that Higgins sought a shift manager job, Tom Simpson, who is white, was hired as brewery manager for the main bottleworks. Soon after he became brewery manager, Simpson started making changes to bring production levels up without increasing costs. One of the changes that he made related to overtime. All of the employees below the level of shift manager had been considered non-exempt for purposes of the Fair Labor Standards Act, which meant that they received overtime pay if they worked more than 40 hours a week. Line supervisors routinely worked between 45 and 50 hours a week because even though they had many of the same duties as the production workers they supervised, they also had to fit in time for some of their supervisory duties. Simpson reclassified the line supervisors as exempt, no longer entitled to overtime pay. At the same time, he raised their wages a bit, but the line supervisors still made on average $25 a week less than they had when they received overtime. In explaining his rationale for the change, Simpson said that the line supervisors were really management, not line workers, and that they should be grateful for the level of responsibility they were given, because "not that long ago, most of you all would have been stuck cleaning the plant. We have come a long way."

Simpson also decided, shortly after he arrived, to withhold wage increases for the two shift managers (who were white), because he thought the bottleworks was performing poorly. In June, Simpson asked Steve Dade, who was working at a small bottleworks in a smaller city a couple of hours away to transfer to the main bottleworks to work as a maintenance supervisor. Shortly after Dade transferred, the other bottleworks was closed for financial reasons. The denial of a pay raise caused the two shift managers to resign in August, which created two open positions. At that time, Randy King was working as a shift manager at a City Brewery bottleworks in a suburb. Simpson asked him to come to the main bottleworks to work as shift manager, and he transferred into that position on September 15. On September 28, Simpson promoted Dade to the other shift manager position. Both King and Dade are white.

John Higgins was a line supervisor at the St. Louis bottleworks prior to the time both shift manager positions became available in August-September. Higgins met with Simpson and expressed a desire to be considered for shift manager. He formally applied on September 1. At the interview, Simpson told Higgins that despite his good work history, to be considered for the shift manager position, he would need a college degree, which Higgins did not have. However, after the first shift manager position was filled by King, Higgins discovered that King did not have a college degree. Higgins asked Simpson about the other position at that time, and Simpson told Higgins he was not going to fill the other shift manager position for six months. Within a couple of weeks, though, he appointed Steve Dade, who also had no college degree. Three other Black men who had been line supervisors in the main bottleworks had also applied for the position of shift manager.

Higgins asked Simpson why he chose King and Dade, and Simpson said that he considered experience in the brewing industry in a successful bottleworks; leadership and organizational skills; experience in more than one plant; having a college degree; and, as the primary consideration, Simpson's belief that it would be better to have as shift managers persons who were not associated with the poorly-performing main facility.

One of the other Black applicants, David Adams, asked Simpson separately why none of the internal applicants were hired. Simpson told Adams that it was because none of the internal applicants applied in time. Higgins didn't remember seeing a posting for the position or hearing about a deadline for applying.

Higgins also said that Simpson was not particularly friendly with any of the Black line supervisors; he spoke and ate lunch with only white employees. Also, several times in the past, Simpson had referred to him and at least one other Black line supervisor as "boys." In a production meeting, Simpson said "Hey, boy" as Higgins was walking through the door. In the cafeteria, Simpson said to another black line supervisor, "Boy, you think you've got enough starch in those jeans?" That supervisor's wife told Simpson that her husband was not a boy, and Simpson laughed.

Evaluate any claims John Higgins may have under Title VII, doing a full legal analysis of those potential claims, and commenting on their strength or weakness. As part of that analysis, identify the arguments City Brewery will make, analyze them, and also evaluate their strength or weakness.

**4.** The City of Townsville Fire Department changed the way it hired firefighters 5 years ago. It had been criticized in the past for the way that hiring was accomplished. It was accused of nepotism and cronyism. Most of the firefighters were white men, and hiring was done at the fire station level. There were only 3 women in the whole department at that time.

Additionally, the fire department had some high profile failed rescues. For example, six years ago, a fire began in a condemned building that a few people had been squatting in—living illegally. Units responded right away, but an older man was trapped on the fifth floor. Three firefighters made it to that location in their heavy gear before the stairs got too dangerous and weak from the fire. Unfortunately, none was strong enough to carry the man, who they found unconscious. They couldn't get him to safety. They were forced to retreat, and the man died of his injuries. Those sorts of emergencies were pretty rare, but there were 3 or 4 similar incidents a year.

The City adopted a new process as a result of these things 5 years ago. It now uses the results of a physical fitness performance test developed and administered then to determine who to hire.

In developing its firefighter performance test, the City hired an expert to conduct a job analysis and design the test. The job analysis identified abilities the expert deemed essential to firefighter job performance and ranked those abilities in order of their importance to firefighter job performance.

According to the City's job analysis, the job of firefighter required a whole range of abilities, including physical abilities, cognitive abilities, and other crucial abilities. It found that the ability most important to the job of firefighter was the ability to make decisions quickly when under pressure. The next most important ability was the ability to remain calm and follow directions when under pressure in an emergency. The third most important ability was the ability to work as part of a team to accomplish a task. Of the ten next most important abilities, only four are the physical abilities the performance test measures. The City's expert determined that there were no standardized tests that can validly measure these sorts of soft skills in this setting, and so limited the test to more concrete physical attributes that are easier to measure.

The test measured agility, endurance, strength, and speed, in combination, through various physical exercises and time limits. The scoring was set from 1 to 100. Most people do not possess all four of these traits in equal amounts. Women tend to excel at agility and to some extent endurance, at least at a minimum level for a long period, while men tend to excel at strength and speed in shorter bursts.

The expert gave the test to the firefighters currently working for the City. Based on the expert's analysis, she determined that an overall score of 65 was a passing score. At 65, most people (90%) could accomplish all of the daily tasks of a firefighter. At that same score, about half of the people (48%) would be able to handle most of the tasks required in the most serious emergency.

The City's Fire Chief, concerned about its emergency responses, asked about a figure that would predict overwhelming success in emergencies. In the words of the Fire Chief, "We're in the business of public safety, and if you're trapped on the roof of a burning building, you don't necessarily want the truck to be filled with the guys who just squeaked by. You want the best chance to be rescued." Thus, the expert also gave the City the results of further findings based on the scores of the current firefighters. The firefighters with the most commendations scored above a 90 on the physical performance test. These were the firefighters most prepared to handle emergency situations.

Based on the expert's analysis, the City set 65 as a cutoff score for passing the physical performance test. Any applicant scoring below 65 is denied any further consideration in the City's hiring process.

Those scoring at or above 65 pass and are rated "qualified" for the position of firefighter. Although all candidates scoring 65 or above are deemed qualified, the City has thus far hired only candidates who achieved a score of 90 or better. As a result, the overwhelming majority of candidates who passed the performance test and were rated by the City as "qualified" based on their scores have been and are continuing to be denied the opportunity to be hired. Moreover, very, very few women scored at this threshold, so few have been hired.

Here are the important figures from when the test was administered 5 years ago:

- Approximately 3,000 total applicants
    - Approximately 1,800 (60%) applicants are men
    - Approximately 1,200 (40%) are women.
- Approximately 2,200 applicants scored at the level of 65 or above.
    - Approximately 1,320 (60%) are men,
    - and approximately 880 (40%) are women
- Approximately 220 applicants scored at the level of 90 or above.
    - Approximately 198 (90%) are male
    - Approximately 22 (10%) are female.

Of the approximately 1,800 male applicants who took the test, approximately 1,320, about 73%, passed. Of the approximately 1,200 female applicants who took the performance test, approximately 880, or about 73%, passed.

Of the approximately 1,320 men who passed, approximately 198 (15%) scored a 90 or above. Of the approximately 880 women who passed, 22 (2.5%) scored a 90 or above.

As a result of using these results, the number of failed rescues has declined significantly to no more than one per year. In addition, the department's diversity has grown. More non-white firefighters have been hired, and more women. The Fire Chief noted, however:

> It's still nowhere near equal, especially for women, but it's better. Women just don't have the strength that men do, I guess. Maybe the women can just train harder to perform at that high level. I don't know what the figures might be on training, but it seems like the problem is with our applicants, not the test. And when lives are at stake, you don't want to take chances.

The Fire Chief also noted that other cities use different processes, but those are costly to develop and administer, and so plans to re-administer this test to create a new list of potential hires.

Ann, Brenda, and Cher are all women who took the test, but received scores in the 80s. As a result, they were on the qualified list, but have not been hired.

If they bring an action after exhausting their administrative remedies (assume that action would be timely based on the announcement that a new list would be generated and thus they would lose their chance to be hired), what claims might they have? What defenses will the City raise? Who is likely to be successful and why?

# Additional Short Answer Questions

1. Title VII and other federal anti-discrimination laws generally require that employers ignore the protected identity characteristics of employees, but there are exceptions to this. What are those exceptions (hint—they are sometimes defenses and sometimes parts of causes of action or causes of action themselves) and how do they allow or even require employers to think about employees' identity characteristics?

2. Mixed motives part 1: Courts have identified two different kinds of disparate treatment cases—pretext cases and mixed motives cases. What do those terms mean?

   Mixed motives part 2: The parties may have preferences for which analysis gets used in any particular case. In other words, sometimes an employee will want his or her case to be analyzed as a pretext case and another employee will want his or her case analyzed as a mixed motives case. Sometimes an employer will want the case analyzed as a pretext case and sometimes a mixed motives case. What facts about a case will drive these preferences? In other words, when will an employee want the case to be a pretext case and when will an employee want the case to be a mixed motives case? And vice versa for the employer?

3. Ann Adams has worked for a McDonalds in St. Louis for ten years. Three years ago, she converted to Pentecostalism. As a member of the Pentecostal church, Adams believes women cannot wear pants. In accordance with this religious belief, Adams has not worn pants, but instead has worn a long skirt, since she converted. Last year, her McDonalds restaurant was bought by Tasty Foods, Inc., which operates several McDonalds franchises. Tasty Foods informed Adams that she had to wear pants to work because of their dress code policy, which requires all employees to wear black pants as part of a standard uniform. Adams explained that she could not wear pants because of her religious beliefs. Tasty Foods fired her for failing to adhere to its dress code policy.

   A. If, after exhausting her administrative remedies, Adams brings an action against Tasty Foods under Title VII, is she likely to survive a motion to dismiss? Explain why or why not in your analysis.

   B. If you represented the employer, what additional factual areas would you want to explore with your client to give it the best chance to succeed at summary judgment? Explain why—what would the legal analysis be?

4. We represent InterActiveCorp (IAC), a holding company that owns Meet, an online dating service, which in turn owns Tenderly, the location-based social search and chat mobile app. IAC is worried about the work environment at Tenderly for the people who run the business and create and support the app.

Tenderly has come under fire for its toxic environment. There is no question that the highest level employees have engaged in actionable sexual harassment, conditioning work benefits on submission to sexual advances, and engaging in other misogynistic, homophobic, and transphobic conduct. The workplace was full of harassment and other manifestations of discrimination.

IAC has asked us to advise it on how to avoid something like this happening in the future—a separate team is handling the current litigation. IAC's goals are not just to avoid liability but also to make its workplace more attractive to diverse candidates.

A. What should an effective harassment policy contain, and what other things, like tone, language or length, are important to consider?

B. What advice would you give to Tenderly about how to implement this policy?

# Answers

Topic 1 Answers

# General Overview of Applicable Law, Enforcement, and Remedies

1.1 Section 705(a) (42 U.S.C. § 2000e-4(a)) of Title VII creates the EEOC and sets the number of commissioners at 5.

1.2 B is the correct answer. Section 705(a) (42 U.S.C. § 2000e-4(a)) provides that "not more than three" commissioners "shall be members of the same political party."

A is not correct because the distinction made by Congress in this section was based on political party, and not the kind of perspective that might be informed by which "side" of the employment relationship a person is on or has experience working for.

C is not correct, in part, because Article III of the Constitution governs judges and other tribunals that adjudicate claims. The EEOC does not adjudicate claims in the private sector. In addition, section 705(a) (42 U.S.C. § 2000e-4(a)) provides for five-year terms, although the appointment may be longer under certain circumstances if there is a delay in appointing a successor or shorter if a person is appointed to fill a vacancy of a commissioner who did not serve a full five-year term.

D is not correct because, while the Senate provides advice and consent to appointments of the Commissioners (who are nominated by the President), there is no provision for the removal of commissioners by Congress.

1.3 C is the correct answer. Section 706(e) of Title VII (42 U.S.C. § 2000e-5(e)) provides that charges must be filed with the EEOC within 180 days after the unlawful employment practice occurred unless the person aggrieved has filed a charge with a state fair employment practices agency that can seek relief for the unfair employment practice. Because Alabama has no state fair employment practices agency, this is the time period in which a person aggrieved must file a charge.

1.4 D is the correct answer. Section 706(e) of Title VII (42 U.S.C. § 2000e-5(e)) provides that when an aggrieved person first files a charge with an appropriate state or local fair employment practices agency, that person has 300 days to file a charge with the EEOC. The EEOC has worksharing agreements with all of the state fair employment practices agencies, and many local agencies, that provide the agencies will cross-file any charges received. In other words, charges first filed with the EEOC will be sent by the EEOC and cross-filed under these agreements with the appropriate state or local agency, and charges first filed with state or local agencies will be sent, or cross-filed, with the EEOC. State laws impose time limits on charges to enforce state antidiscrimination law, and missing the state's deadline may affect the availability of state law remedies. Those limits, however, are irrelevant for purposes of Title VII. *EEOC v. Commercial Office Products Co.*, 486 U.S. 108 (1988).

**1.5** A is the best answer. Although sections 706(c) and (e)(1) (42 U.S.C. §2000e-5(c), (e)(1)) provide that a charge must first be filed with a state or local fair employment practices agency (if there is one) and that the EEOC must wait for sixty days after that charge has been filed to begin its proceedings, the time period can be shortened or waived. Title VII provides that EEOC's processes can begin as soon as state proceedings are terminated. As a matter of practice, the worksharing agreements between the EEOC and state or local fair employment practices agencies provide that the EEOC can begin its proceedings immediately without waiting. *EEOC v. Commercial Office Products Co.*, 486 U.S. 108 (1988).

**1.6** B is the best answer. Section 706(b) (42 U.S.C. §2000e-5(b)) provides that if the Commission, after an investigation, determines that there is not reasonable cause to believe that the charge is true, the Commission should dismiss the charge. Section 706(f) (42 U.S.C. §2000e-5(f)) provides that if a charge is dismissed, the person who filed the charge can seek a right to sue letter, and then file a lawsuit in a state or federal court. Section 706(g) provides that the court will decide whether an unlawful employment practice has occurred and does not suggest that the EEOC process should be given deference. The process is not judicial review of the agency's decision, and in fact, under section 709(e) (42 U.S.C. §2000e-8), the EEOC may not make public any information obtained by the Commission in its investigation.

A is not completely accurate. Although the charge would be dismissed, the matter is not closed, since the person can bring an action in court.

C is not correct because Title VII does not set up a system of judicial review of the EEOC's decision or require deference to it.

D is not correct because the rules of res judicata are not satisfied and state and federal courts are treated the same for purposes of enforcement.

**1.7** C is the correct answer. Section 706(f) (42 U.S.C. §2000e-5(f)) provides that a civil action can be brought by the person aggrieved within ninety days after receiving notice that the EEOC has not entered into a conciliation agreement with the respondent or that no action will be brought in response to the charge.

**1.8** **D** is the correct answer. Section 706(f) (42 U.S.C. § 2000e-5(f)) does not put a time limit on the EEOC's investigation but provides that, if no decision has been reached on a charge within 180 days, a right to sue notice should be issued to the aggrieved person. An investigation could go on longer, and this time period could also be extended for purposes of cross-filing under subsections (c) and (d) of that provision.

**1.9** **A**, **B**, and **E** are all expressly prohibited by Title VII. Section 703(a)(1) (42 U.S.C. § 2000e-2(a)(1)) prohibits employers from making decisions about hiring because of race, and section 703(a)(2) and (k) (42 U.S.C. §§ 2000e-2(a)(2), 2(k)) prohibit employers from relying on practices that have the effect of excluding members of one race unless those practices are job related and consistent with business necessity. Lastly, section 704(b) (42 U.S.C. § 2000e-3(b)) prohibits printing an ad that indicates the employer intends to engage in an unlawful employment practice. Basing a hiring decision on the sex of the applicant is a violation unless sex is a bona fide occupational qualification for that position.

**C** and **D** are commonly believed to violate Title VII, but they do not. People tend to think that those questions are discriminatory, because they suggest that the speaker would use the information to discriminate. Title VII does not prohibit asking any questions, although questions like these would be circumstantial evidence of a Title VII violation. In addition, some state laws do expressly prohibit asking certain questions.

**1.10** **C**, **F**, and **G** are correct. Section 703 (42 U.S.C. § 2000e-2) defines unfair employment practices which can be engaged in by employers (a), labor unions (c), and employment agencies (b). Section 701(b) (42 U.S.C. § 2000e(b)) defines an employer as "a person engaged in an industry affecting commerce who has fifteen or more employees" for a specified period of time. Other federal and state statutes prohibit the discrimination described in the other letters except for **B**. Private membership clubs are generally not prohibited from discriminating.

**1.11** **C** and **G** are correct. Section 4 (29 U.S.C. § 623) of the ADEA parallels Title VII in its focus on employers, labor unions, and employment agencies. Section 11(b) (29 U.S.C. § 630(b)) limits coverage to employers of 20 or more employees, however. And section 13(a) (29 U.S.C. § 631(a)) defines the protected class as people 40 years old and older.

**1.12** **B**, **D**, and **E** are correct. Section 101(2) (42 U.S.C. § 12111(2)) of the ADA parallels Title VII and the ADEA in covered entities, and, like Title VII, section 101(5)(A) (42 U.S.C. § 12111(5)(A)) provides that it applies to employers who have 15 employees or more.

**1.13** **C** is the best answer. In *Fort Bend County v. Davis*, 139 S. Ct. 1843 (2019), the Supreme Court held that the filing of a charge with the EEOC is not a jurisdictional requirement.

Plaintiffs are required to exhaust their administrative remedies, which, for purposes of this hypothetical, would likely require the plaintiff to include their religion claim in their timely filed charge. *See Bryant v. Bell Atl. Med., Inc.*, 288 F.3d 124, 132 (4th Cir. 2002) (limiting viable claims to those that could reasonably be reflected to flow from the charge filed). But because the exhaustion requirement is not jurisdictional, a defendant can waive the right to use it as a defense by litigating. Because the employer here fully litigated the claim and failed to raise exhaustion before the trial court, it almost certainly waived its right to do so. That was the factual scenario in *Fort Bend County*.

**A** is not correct because Title VII does not create a substantive right for employers to an investigation that due process could protect.

**B** is not correct because, even though exhaustion is required and the employee arguably did not exhaust the religion claim, the employer almost certainly waived that claim by not raising it until the appeal.

**D** is not correct because there is no harmless error doctrine like the one described for employment discrimination claims that would allow a court to consider claims it lacked jurisdiction over as long as it had jurisdiction over some.

**1.14** **C** is the best answer. To be covered by Title VII, an employer must have at least 15 employees. This employer clearly has ten and likely no more. Partners are not likely to be employees, because they are often, essentially, owners. The test for whether a person is an employee is guided by part of the common law test: whether the person is subject to another's control or right to control the details of work. Partners are not automatically owners and can be employees under this test. *Clackamas Gastroenterology Assocs. v. Wells*, 538 U.S. 440 (2003) (adopting the EEOC's test for employees in an ADA case).

**A** is not correct because it is not clear that the clinic has 15 or more employees, since the partners may not be employees.

**B** is not correct because, even though Chris is clearly an employee and there are more than 15 workers, the statute requires 15 *employees*.

**D** is not the best answer. It is possible that there are there are not enough employees to satisfy Title VII's coverage requirements, but unless we know more about these partners, we don't know whether they are employees.

**1.15** The answer would not be different if Chris were fired for being 40 years old. The same test would apply, since the Court has adopted the common law test in a variety of employment contexts and the EEOC has adopted it, at least in part, as well. Moreover the ADEA has a *larger* requirement—20 employees.

**1.16** The answer would not be different if Chris were fired because of a disability. That would be directly governed by *Clackamas*, which was an ADA case, and the employee threshold in Title I of the ADA is the same as Title VII—15.

1.17 B is the best answer. Even though the employer here is a covered employer, Blair is likely not an employee. The test for whether a worker is an employee is, in part, whether the person is subject to another's control or right to control the details of work. *Clackamas Gastroenterology Assocs. v. Wells*, 538 U.S. 440 (2003). An unpaid intern may very well satisfy this test, although if they are substantially supervised by their educational institution, that may dilute the control the putative employer would be considered to have. *See Cuddeback v. Florida Bd. of Educ.*, 381 F.3d 1230, 1234-35 (11th Cir. 2004). More importantly, unpaid interns are often considered a type of volunteer. The EEOC has indicated in guidance that to be considered an employee, a worker must receive "significant remuneration." *See* EEOC, Compliance Manual, Section 2: Threshold Issues, § 2-III.A.1.c, http://www.eeoc.gov/policy/docs/threshold.html. If the University provides that remuneration in the form of benefits, the intern may be an employee of their placement, but course credit has not been considered to be enough. *See Jacob-Mua v. Veneman*, 289 F.3d 517, 521 (8th Cir. 2002) (abrogated on other grounds by *Torgerson v. City of Rochester*, 643 F.3d 1031 (2011) (en banc)).

A is not correct because interns can be employees if they receive significant remuneration and otherwise satisfy the right to control test.

C is not correct. Even though harassment is a form of discrimination, Title VII only prohibits discrimination against employees.

D is not correct because Title VII does not cover the educational relationship.

1.18 A is the best answer. As an associate, Alex is an employee, and section 703(a)(1) (42 U.S.C. § 2000e-2(a)(1)) prohibits sex discrimination in "compensation, terms, conditions, or privileges of employment." Even though partners may not be employees, promotion to partner has been held to be a term, condition, or privilege of employment. *Hishon v. King & Spalding*, 467 U.S. 69 (1984).

B is not correct because section 703 does not list denial of a promotion explicitly. It mentions hiring, discharge and discrimination in "compensation, terms, conditions, or privileges of employment" as a catch-all.

C is not correct because, even though partners may not be employees, they may be if they satisfy the right to control test. *Clackamas Gastroenterology Assocs. v. Wells*, 538 U.S. 440 (2003). Additionally, the opportunity to be promoted to partner is a benefit used to recruit associates, and so can be a term, condition, or privilege of employment.

D is not correct. Law firms may be employers covered by Title VII even if they are partnerships. Partnerships as legal entities often have employees in addition to partners, and if a partnership has enough employees, it will be covered.

1.19 A is the best answer. 42 U.S.C. § 1981 provides, in part,

> All persons within the jurisdiction of the United States shall have the same right in every State and Territory to make and enforce contracts . . . as is enjoyed by white citizens . . . .

The employment relationship is considered a contractual relationship even when there is no written contract and the relationship can be terminated at will by either party. *See Johnson v. Railway Express Agency*, 421 U.S. 454 (1975).

B is not factually correct. The plaintiffs in those cases did not have written employment contracts.

C is not correct because § 1981 does not mention employment.

D is not correct. Although § 1981 was enacted as part of the Civil Rights Act of 1866 to enforce the Thirteenth and Fourteenth Amendments, it is not limited to redressing "the badges and incidents of slavery" the way that the Thirteenth Amendment itself is. So even if race discrimination in employment would be considered is a badge or incident of slavery, it need not be to fall under the protection of the statute.

**1.20** A, B, and C are correct. Section 706 (42 U.S.C. § 2000e-5) provides the mechanism for Title VII's enforcement. In it, the Commission is given the power to investigate charges (b), and if it determines that there is reasonable cause to believe that the charge is true, "shall endeavor to eliminate" that discrimination "by informal methods of conference, conciliation, and persuasion." If the Commission can't "secure from the respondent a conciliation agreement acceptable to the Commission," it can bring a civil action against the respondent (f), as long as the respondent isn't a state or local government entity. The Commission also has a few additional, related powers, like the power to intervene in an action brought by the charging party, and powers to make technical studies and provide education and outreach assistance. It can also refer *civil* cases to the Attorney General where the defendant is a state or local government entity. The Commission does not have other powers that federal agencies sometimes have, like the power to adjudicate claims (although it does serve as an appellate body for federal sector discrimination claims) or impose fines or cease and desist orders. And, although not listed, the Commission does not have the power to issue substantive rules under Title VII, only procedural rules.

**1.21** C, D, E, and F are correct. What relief can a successful plaintiff get in a disparate impact suit? Section 706(g) (42 U.S.C. § 2000e-5(g)) provides that courts can enjoin an unlawful employment practice and award other affirmative relief including, at least, reinstatement or hiring, backpay, and any other equitable relief appropriate. Subsection (k) further provides that a prevailing party can get a reasonable attorney's fee and costs. Fees and costs are also allowed pursuant to 42 U.S.C. § 1988. 42 U.S.C. § 1981a limits compensatory damages and punitive damages to cases of intentional discrimination, and not disparate impact discrimination.

**1.22** All of the forms of relief listed can be awarded a successful disparate treatment plaintiff under 42 U.S.C. §§ 1981a, 1988, 2000e-5(g), (k).

**1.23** Under Title VII, the Commission is empowered to issue only procedural rules. 42 U.S.C. § 2000e-12(a). The Commission can provide interpretations or opinions that relate to the substance of Title VII, but they do not have a binding effect except that they provide a safe harbor for covered entities that comply with them. *Id.* § 2000e-12(b). Under Title I of the ADA, the Commission has substantive rulemaking power. 42 U.S.C. § 12116.

**1.24** This statement is **False**. Section 703(n) (42 U.S.C. § 2000e-2(n)) provides that "an employment practice that implements and is within the scope of a litigated or consent judgment . . . may not be challenged . . . in a claim under the Constitution or Federal civil rights laws" in most circumstances.

**1.25** C is the best answer. Although Title VII does define employer to include agents of the employer, the circuit courts to consider the issue have held that Title VII does not create individual liability. Rather, the liable entity is the employer.

A is not correct. The fact pattern does describe quid pro quo harassment. However quid pro quo harassment does not result in automatic liability, necessarily, and not liability for individuals.

B is not correct. Although Title VII defines employer to include agents of the employer, it has not been held to create individual liability for those agents.

D is not correct because, when harassment culminates in a tangible employment action, an employee's failure to follow an anti-harassment policy will not be a defense.

# Analytical Frameworks: Disparate Treatment and Disparate Impact Basics

2.1 The main difference between disparate treatment and disparate impact is that disparate treatment is said to be "intentional," and described as requiring a motive to treat someone differently because they are a member of a protected class. Disparate impact focuses on the effect of an employment practice. An employer doesn't have to intend that that members of a protected class be affected or even know about the different effects.

2.2 A is the best answer. Although the fact pattern has a lot of information about the demographics of the city, the key facts are that the company assigns white employees to one location and Black employees to another. This is intentional disparate treatment. The fact that the reason for this disparate treatment is based on a potentially benign reason—an assumption about customer preference—does not change the fact that the choice of location is based on the race of the employee.

B is not correct because it is not the segregation that is causing the effect, it's the employer's choice to have assignments match the racial segregation.

C is not correct for two reasons. First, race can never be a bona fide occupational qualification under Title VII. Only sex, religion, and in narrow circumstances, national origin can be. Second, customer preference cannot make a protected class be a bona fide occupational qualification. Allowing customer preference to justify intentional discrimination would nullify Title VII—it would insulate discrimination too easily.

D is not correct. Business necessity is a defense to disparate impact, but this is disparate treatment. Moreover, the employer does not have evidence that assigning by race is necessary for selling financial products or brokerage services. It simply relies on an assumption that this would be true. That is not enough to demonstrate that a practice is job related and consistent with business necessity. Finally, a benign reason for disparate treatment, or a further purpose that disparate treatment is meant to serve, does not change the fact that the employer has engaged in disparate treatment and does not provide a defense.

2.3 C is the best answer. The facts clearly say that the reason the HR director doesn't hire Aron is because of age, and Aron is in the class protected by the ADEA.

A is not correct. Students often confuse the question of liability with questions about conclusive proof, and it can be challenging to accept an "omniscient" view of the decisionmaker. It's a good thing, in lawyering terms, to worry about how a state of mind will be proven, but the question does not ask about that practical challenge. And for lawyers who are in-house or who represent employers, thinking about what creates liability is essential for counseling clients.

**B** is not correct. Animus is generally not required for disparate treatment liability. Simply relying on age is the intent required.

**D** is not correct because the ADEA does not require employers to prefer older people. It is fine for age to be irrelevant to the employer's decision.

2.4 **B** is the best answer. The State agency is using veteran status to make a decision. Although women are affected by the policy, veteran status is not itself a class protected by Title VII (although state *laws* creating a veteran's preference are exempt from application of Title VII under section 712 (42 U.S.C. § 2000e-11)), and so the preference is sex-neutral. Neutral policies with disparate effects may cause an unlawful disparate impact, but if the policy is job related and consistent with business necessity, the disparity will not violate Title VII. 42 U.S.C. § 2000e-2(a)(2), (k).

**A** is not correct because states and their agencies are "persons" who can engage in an industry affecting commerce and have fifteen or more employees under section 701(a) and (b) (42 U.S.C. § 2000e(a), (b)). Thus, state agencies can be employers.

**C** is not correct. Even though the sex-based disparity is very large, that disparity by itself is not disparate treatment, and even knowledge of the disparity doesn't make this disparate treatment. Only if the reason the agency picked veteran's status was because they wanted to use it as a proxy for sex in order to exclude women would the choice be disparate treatment. *Personnel Administrator of Massachusetts v. Feeney*, 442 U.S. 256 (1979).

**D** is not the best answer. While it is true that veterans are not a protected class under Title VII and that plays a role in why this scenario is disparate impact, the better answer (B) lays out the full rule for disparate impact.

2.5 **A** is the best answer. Even though disparate impact and disparate treatment may seem to be entirely different types of discrimination, they are not necessarily incompatible in a lawsuit. The disparate treatment framework seeks to prove that the decisionmakers were motivated by the protected class to make the decision they did. Here, using that framework, Ana could argue that Elm Park chose to prefer residents because doing so would allow them to hire mostly white applicants. She would argue that residency is a pretext for race discrimination, because residency was being used as a proxy for race. Alternatively, Ana could forego having to prove that the reason Elm Park chose the residency preference was because of the racial effect, and simply prove the effect, believing that Elm Park will be unable to show that the residency preference is job related and consistent with business necessity.

**B** is not the best answer because the statistical evidence would almost certainly show that the residency preference has the effect of excluding Black potential applicants at a rate disproportional to their numbers in the eligible labor pool.

**C** is not the best answer because Ana could use these facts to argue that the use of the residential preference is a pretext for discrimination on the basis of race. There is nothing in the fact pattern that precludes this argument.

**D** is not the best answer because these facts could support either a disparate impact or disparate treatment claim, as explained above.

**2.6** If Ana brings this claim under § 1981, then she will only be able to bring it as a disparate treatment claim. Section 1981 enforces the Reconstruction Amendments, and so actions are a little more limited than under Title VII. Section 1981 applies to private parties, and not just state action, because of the 13th amendment. However, it only reaches disparate treatment and not disparate impact. So if Ana brought this claim under § 1981, **B** would be the best answer.

**2.7** **D** is the best answer because it is the only option that uses the correct language for a defense to either disparate treatment or disparate impact, and it is not foreclosed by the facts. If Ana brought a disparate impact cause of action, Elm Park could prevail if it could show that the residency preference satisfies the business necessity defense. Although D does not provide a defense to a disparate treatment claim, and so isn't a perfect answer, none of the other three options provide a correct and complete defense to either kind of claim.

**A** is not the best answer because, even though it provides an accurate statement of what Elm Park would say to rebut Ana's prima facie case in a disparate treatment action, it is not a complete statement of what Elm Park's defense strategy would be. Elm Park would also have to argue that Ana had not proven or could not prove that this reason was a pretext for race discrimination. In other words, simply articulating a nondiscriminatory reason does not guarantee a win for Elm Park. Ana must also be unable to prove that the reason is a pretext for discrimination.

**B** is not the best answer because it frames the Bona Fide Occupational Qualification defense incorrectly. The BFOQ defense provides that in some circumstances, the protected class itself can be a BFOQ. Here, that would require Elm Park to say that being white is a BFOQ. Moreover, race and color cannot be BFOQs. So, this defense is unavailable.

**C** is not the best answer because it does not provide a defense to disparate impact. To determine whether there is a disparate impact, those in the job must be compared to the eligible labor pool. The student body is not the eligible labor pool.

**2.8** **D** is the best answer. This question is testing the difference between disparate treatment and disparate impact in a scenario like the one in *UAW v. Johnson Controls*, 499 U.S. 187 (1991). Because the policy distinguishes on the basis of sex (in addition to fertility), it is an explicit sex-based distinction that can only be defended using the Bona Fide Occupational Qualification defense.

**A** is not correct because it provides the defense for disparate impact.

**B** is not correct because any distinction on the basis of sex, even one for benign reasons, is disparate treatment (unless that distinction is part of a valid affirmative action plan).

**C** is not correct because undue hardship is not a defense to disparate treatment on the basis of sex.

**2.9** **A** is the best answer. This question, too, is testing the difference between disparate treatment and disparate impact. Zip codes here are correlated with race, but there are no facts that suggest that this correlation is the reason that Eon Corp. adopted the preference. Instead, it seems to be relying on a neutral criterion that has a race-based effect. Thus, this is disparate impact, and business necessity is the defense for it. A gives the business necessity defense.

**B** is incorrect because "reasonable factor other than race" is not a defense.

**C** is incorrect because it uses BFOQ, which is the defense to disparate treatment.

**D** is incorrect because accommodation is not a defense, and is not relevant to a race discrimination claim.

Topic 3 **Answers**

# Disparate Treatment, the *McDonnell Douglas* Test, and other Frameworks

3.1 A is the best answer. In *Reeves v. Sanderson Plumbing Products, Inc.*, 530 U.S. 133 (2000), the Court made clear that even though the presumption of discrimination drops out once the employer provides a nondiscriminatory reason for its actions, a permissible inference of discrimination remains. In that case, the Court was clarifying its prior holdings in *McDonnell Douglas v. Green*, 411 U.S. 792 (1973), *Texas Department of Community Affairs v. Burdine*, 450 U.S. 248 (1981), and *St. Mary's Honor Center v. Hicks*, 509 U.S. 502 (1993), which had created some confusion. Because the prima facie case is viewed by some as "thin," there had been concern over using those facts to conclude that the decisionmaker based their decision on the person's protected class. The prima facie case is flexible; it requires only that a plaintiff prove that they are a member of a protected class, that they were qualified for the position or performing adequately, that they suffered an adverse employment action, and, for hiring, that the employer kept looking for someone with the plaintiff's qualifications or did hire someone with the plaintiff's qualifications. Despite these concerns, the Court made clear that proving this creates an inference of discrimination because employers had to have *some* reason for their action, and if the plaintiff proves that the most common reasons were not relied on, a reasonable trier of fact could conclude that the reason was the plaintiff's protected class.

B is not the best answer because the Court in *Reeves* affirmatively rejected that position, which was one side of a circuit split that developed after *Hicks*. That position was referred to as "pretext-plus."

C is not correct because, as *McDonnell Douglas* and *Burdine* made clear, the plaintiff must have an opportunity to prove that the reason offered is a pretext for discrimination.

D is not correct because it describes instead the result of either a disparate impact action, or possibly a successful defense to a mixed motives case, where the plaintiff proves that their protected class played a role in the adverse action, and the defendant successfully proves that it would have made the same decision without considering the protected class.

3.2 C is the best answer. This is simply another way to ask question 3.1. It describes the effect of the presumption dropping out of the analysis, but the inference remaining, coupled with proof that the employer lied.

**A** is not correct because the Court held in *Hicks* that the act of providing evidence, even if not believed, still counts to discharge the employer's burden. That result was viewed as necessary to ensure that the burden of persuasion, a part of the burden of proof, remained with the plaintiff throughout.

**B** is not correct because it describes the pretext-plus position that the Court rejected in *Reeves*. Requiring additional, more conclusive proof would put too heavy a burden on plaintiffs, who lack access to information about the decisionmaker's reasoning. The reason for shifting the burden of production to defendants if plaintiffs can prove a prima facie case is because, under the at-will rule, literally *any reason other than the plaintiff's protected class* will mean no liability. An employer can refuse to hire or can fire someone "for a good reason, a bad reason, or no reason at all," just not a reason that violates Title VII. It's nearly impossible to disprove every potential good and bad reason. Requiring articulation of a nondiscriminatory reason allows the plaintiff to focus in and disprove that one thing.

**D** is not the best answer. The Court has made clear, repeatedly, that direct evidence of discrimination is not required to prove discrimination.

3.3 **B** is the best answer. As the Court clarified in *Swierkiewicz v. Sorema*, 534 U.S. 506 (2002), the function of a *McDonnell Douglas*-style prima facie case is for a plaintiff with circumstantial evidence to have to produce enough evidence to warrant shifting the burden of production to the defendant to provide evidence that it relied on a nondiscriminatory reason for its conduct. At a motion to dismiss stage, the only question is whether the alleged facts, if true, show a plausible claim that the defendant took an adverse employment action against the plaintiff because of the plaintiff's protected class. Similarly, after all of the evidence is in and after a jury verdict, both, the only question is whether, based on all of the evidence, a rational jury could conclude that the defendant took an adverse employment action against the plaintiff because of the plaintiff's protected class. It's only at the summary judgment stage (of these options) that the sufficiency of the prima facie case can be challenged, because the question there is whether the plaintiff can provide enough evidence to warrant the employer having any burden at all.

3.4 **A** is the best answer here. As part of his case, no matter what proof structure he uses, Ellis must show that he suffered an adverse employment action. If he did not, then summary judgment should be granted to the employer. Ellis's territory was changed, but no other terms or conditions of his work were changed. At first glance, this might not appear to be enough of an adverse action to warrant Title VII protection. It was not hiring, firing, a promotion, a demotion, discipline, or a pay decision. It was not a change to the number of packages he had to deliver, and it wasn't directly a change to his hours. However, functionally, his hours were increased, which means that pay was reduced. Imagine that he made \$160 per day. Before the change, that was \$20 per hour. After the change, it is a reduced rate, to about \$17.78 per hour. Additionally, his working conditions may have become more arduous by adding more driving. *See Minor v. Centocor, Inc.*, 457 F.3d 632 (2006) (holding that an increase in hours and functional decrease in rate of pay caused by larger territory was an adverse employment action).

B is not the best answer. Although the fact pattern relied on a stereotype related to Latinos in making its decision, which is direct evidence that Package Express relied on Ellis's race or national origin to make the change to his route, that is evidence of motive/causation alone. Ellis still has to be able to provide evidence that would show that he suffered an adverse employment action to survive summary judgment.

C is not the best answer because changing the number of packages to be delivered would be just one type of adverse action that could have occurred. Many different kinds of adverse actions could have been taken, and the facts suggest an alternative potential adverse action—that the increase in territory caused an increase in working hours and decrease in hourly rate of pay.

D is not correct. Title VII protects decisions about hiring, firing, promotions, pay, and discipline, but it uses the more open-ended terms of discrimination in "terms, conditions, or privileges of employment," as well.

3.5 B is the best answer. A comparator is a person to compare the plaintiff to. For an inference of discrimination to be made from comparator evidence, the comparator must be similar to the plaintiff. If they are similar, but differed in protected class, and were treated differently, a fact-finder can draw a conclusion that protected class was the reason for the different treatment.

3.6 C is the best answer. There isn't a single framework that has to be used to prove disparate treatment, but if a plaintiff is using qualifications evidence, they are likely using the *McDonnell Douglas* framework in some form, and part of that prima facie case, in a hiring or promotion case, generally requires a plaintiff to prove that they are qualified for the position they were seeking. Once a plaintiff proves a prima facie case and the defendant articulates a nondiscriminatory reason, the plaintiff must prove that reason is a pretext for discrimination. The Court has repeatedly held that a plaintiff can prove pretext in a wide variety of ways.

A is not the correct answer because this is the language the Court explicitly rejected in *Ash v. Tyson Foods*, 546 U.S. 454 (2006).

B is not the best answer. If qualifications evidence is the *only* evidence of pretext that a plaintiff has, then this statement would be true. However, it is not as complete a statement of the law as C.

D is not the best answer for a similar reason. If the plaintiff is substantially more qualified than the person who was awarded the position, that may be enough for a reasonable jury to find in the plaintiff's favor.

3.7 **B** is the best answer. The Court of Appeals in *Reeves* used the "pretext-plus" standard to evaluate Reeves's claim. It ignored the Courts' language in prior cases that proof of a prima facie case plus proof that would allow the factfinder to disbelieve the employer's reason would allow a reasonable factfinder to infer that discrimination was the real reason. This was part of a circuit split that developed after *St. Mary's Honor Center v. Hicks*. There, the plaintiff proved a prima facie case and also proved the reason given was not true. While the trier of fact there could have inferred that discrimination was the real reason, the judge did not infer that and instead concluded that a different, nondiscriminatory reason was the motive. The key in these cases is that as long as there is proof of prima facie case and proof that casts doubt on the employer's reason, the actual finding of the factfinder will almost certainly be reasonable and cannot be second-guessed by an appellate court.

**A** is not correct because the Court of Appeals recognized that the trier of fact had reasonably disbelieved the employer's non-discriminatory reason. The Court of Appeals just held that was not enough.

**C** is not correct because the Court of Appeals recognized that the trier of fact had reasonably found that Reeves was replaced by younger employees, so he did have comparators.

**D** is not correct. Although the Court of Appeals would have required more evidence, that evidence did not have to be direct evidence of age discrimination.

3.8 **A** is the best answer. This is a classic example of a comparator case and key to understanding exactly what antidiscrimination law prohibits. Remember that ordinarily, an employer can fire a person for a good reason, like theft, but also for no reason, and even for a bad reason. But if the reason is race, the employer will be liable. Here, the employer asserted that the theft was the reason for the discharge, but the same theft wasn't serious enough to discharge the other employees, and the only difference between them in the record before the court was their race. But for his race, the plaintiff would not have been fired for theft.

**B** is not correct. Suggesting that a de minimis injury would not justify termination suggests that an employer must have a sufficiently weighty reason or cause for the discharge. That is not what the at-will, default rule provides.

**C** is not correct. The facts suggested that the employer was motivated by the plaintiff's race. That is disparate treatment.

**D** is not correct. Business necessity is a defense to disparate impact, not disparate treatment. And this is not an accurate statement of the business necessity test, because it doesn't mention job-relatedness.

3.9 **C** is the best answer. These are the core facts of *Price Waterhouse v. Hopkins*, 490 U.S. 228 (1989), and describe a mixed motives case. Mixed motives means that the decisionmaker had both discriminatory and nondiscriminatory reasons for its decision. In this hypothetical, the motives were mixed because there were multiple decisionmakers, some with discriminatory motives and others without. A single decisionmaker can also have multiple motives. Title

VII provides that if the plaintiff proves that their protected class was a motivating factor, the defendant will be liable. It can avoid damages and some types of equitable relief if it can prove that it would have made the same decision without considering the plaintiff's protected class. 42 U.S.C. § 2000e-2(k). This question can seem a little tricky because this wasn't exactly the result in *Price Waterhouse*. Mixed motives was recognized, but the language for what, exactly, a plaintiff had to prove was not clear, and if the employer proved it would have made the same decision regardless, it would be relieved of liability. The Civil Rights Act of 1991 adopted the language that now governs and provides for liability regardless.

**A** is not correct. As long as the plaintiff's protected class also motivated the employer, it will have violated Title VII. Having one nondiscriminatory reason does not insulate a discriminatory reason unless the employer can prove that the discriminatory reason *was not* a but-for reason.

**B** is not correct. Some partners are employees if they are subject to sufficient control. *Clackamas Gastroenterology Assocs. v. Wells*, 538 U.S. 440 (2003). Moreover, promotion to partner can be a term, condition, or privilege of employment. *Hishon v. King & Spalding*, 467 U.S. 69 (1984).

**D** is not the best answer. Hopkins presented expert evidence that the partners who relied on concerns about her treatment of support staff were acting on stereotyped thinking, essentially making assumptions about Hopkins when they didn't have first-hand knowledge of her interactions. But the district court did not accept that and found that concerns about treatment of support staff were nondiscriminatory and were legitimate in the sense that they were believed in good faith by those who expressed them.

**3.10** Mixed motives liability is not available under the ADEA. Ann would have to prove that but for her age, she would have been promoted. *Gross v. FBL Financial Services*, 557 U.S. 167 (2009).

**3.11** **A** is the best answer. This question is testing a couple of different things: rules on comparative qualifications evidence, and the role of the *McDonnell Douglas* proof structure in the ultimate question of discrimination. The rule for the ultimate question of discrimination is expressed by A: looking at all of the evidence as a whole, could a reasonable jury conclude that this decisionmaker was motivated by the plaintiff's race? Here, the question about Fred's feelings, given his race, suggest that Fred's race was an important consideration for the decisionmaker. He wasn't clearly *less* qualified than the person who was hired, so it was probably not his qualifications that made him less attractive. Additionally, the very small number of Black employees could suggest that the employer could routinely be discriminating. Note that a reasonable jury could also find that the decisionmaker was not motivated by race—this evidence doesn't *compel* a single conclusion. But that is not the test.

**B** is not the best answer because it does not reflect the rule for the ultimate legal question. The term of art "manifest imbalance" is used in the systemic disparate treatment context, the affirmative action context, and sometimes the disparate impact context. In at least this context, it is just one piece of evidence that by itself does not necessarily get the case to the jury.

C is not the best answer. Plaintiffs do not necessarily have to prove that they are *more* qualified, but can prove their case with a variety of circumstantial evidence. *Ash v. Tyson Foods*, 546 U.S. 454 (2006).

D is not the best evidence. Plaintiffs can prove pretext in a variety of ways, and aren't limited to proving a lie, per se. A plaintiff can cast doubt that their protected class made a difference by pointing to other affirmative evidence about race in the workplace. *Ash v. Tyson Foods*, 546 U.S. 454 (2006).

**3.12** D is the best answer. This fact pattern is similar to the "cat's paw" case of *Staub v. Proctor Hospital*, 562 U.S. 411 (2011), where the Court adopted the proximate cause test that, where a non-decisionmaker has discriminatory intent, intends to cause an adverse employment action on that ground, and is the proximate cause of that adverse employment action, the employer will be liable for the discrimination even if the actual decisionmaker did not harbor that intent or even know about it. This could be another type of mixed motives case, but instead of using the usual mixed motives framework, the Court created a new one to account for the fact that the person with discriminatory intent lacked direct power from the employer to cause the adverse employment action.

A is not the best answer because good faith by the decisionmaker does not remove the causal effect of the discriminatory intent from the process. *See Staub v. Proctor Hospital*, 562 U.S. 411 (2011).

B is not the best answer because atheism, and freedom from religion, is protected by Title VII's prohibition on discrimination on the grounds of religion. *EEOC v. Townley Eng'g & Mfg. Co.*, 859 F.2d 610, 614-21 (9th Cir. 1988).

C is not the best answer. Although employees cannot be coerced for religious reasons, the fact pattern does not show that the supervisor attempted to make Evelyn engage in a religious practice, profess a religious belief, or adopt a religious belief.

**3.13** C is the best answer. In *Swierkiewicz v. Sorema*, 534 U.S. 506 (2002), the Supreme Court held that a complaint need not follow the format of the *McDonnell Douglas* analytical framework. It just has to plead facts, which if true, would allow a reasonable factfinder to conclude that a reason for the adverse action was the plaintiff's protected class. Here, the evidence all together would allow, although not compel, a reasonable factfinder to conclude that Finn's non-binary gender was the reason they were not promoted.

**A** is incorrect because *McDonnell Douglas* is not the only framework available in circumstantial cases, and it need not be used at the complaint stage even if it will be employed later.

**B** is not correct because comparator evidence is not required.

**D** is not correct because the employer has only the burden of pleading at the motion to dismiss stage, and not the burden of production.

**3.14** **A** is the best answer. Shifting employer reasons can be evidence of pretext, and when taken together with all of the other evidence about how her supervisor's behavior changed when Grace reported her pregnancy, could lead a reasonable factfinder to believe that Grace's pregnancy was the reason for her termination.

**B** is not correct. There is no such presumption.

**C** is not correct. Comparators are not required.

**D** is not correct because it does not negate an inference that the supervisor only began to view Grace's work badly because Grace was pregnant.

Topic 4 Answers

# Defense to Disparate Treatment: BFOQ

**4.1** C is the best answer. This fact pattern demonstrates national origin discrimination. The reason for not hiring Juan is that his nation of origin, i.e., the nation where he was born, was not mainland China. This violates Title VII unless being born in mainland China is a bona fide occupational qualification for the position in question. Authenticity can make national origin a bona fide occupational qualification, but the skill of cooking (the job at issue) is not dependent on country of origin. Cooking is a skill that can be learned.

A is incorrect because business necessity is the defense to disparate impact, and this was disparate treatment.

B is not correct because national origin is what must be the BFOQ. Some attribute or ability might make national origin a BFOQ, but that attribute itself is not the BFOQ meant by this defense.

D is not correct because, even though there is substantial conceptual overlap between race and national origin as a matter of ethnic heritage, the fact pattern is tailored not to ethnicity, but literally country of birth. A person could be any race and be born in mainland China. Also, this answer seems to make a bunch of assumptions about how people's identities make them behave and how motive works. It is possible that Wei also was motivated by race, but that does not negate the fact that he was motivated by national origin.

**4.2** A is the best answer. The fire department here is acting on a descriptive sex stereotype, which is broadly true. It is using sex as a proxy for the attribute it desires. That is disparate treatment and will violate Title VII unless sex is a BFOQ. Because some women are strong enough to carry heavy equipment (and that qualification, too, may be problematic for different reasons), and many men are not strong enough, sex is not a BFOQ. The fire department could instead test directly for strength.

B is not the best answer. The fire department here is using sex itself, not a neutral practice that tends to exclude members of one sex. B would be the best answer if the fire department had a strength requirement, rather than a sex requirement, but the strength requirement tended to exclude women disproportionately.

C is not the best answer, because it does not phrase the rule correctly. Sex must be the BFOQ.

D is not the best answer because employers cannot rely on stereotypes to make a decision regardless of whether those stereotypes are prescriptive (how people of that group ought to behave) or descriptive (what is statistically true about that group). *City Department of Water & Power v. Manhart*, 435 U.S. 702 (1978).

4.3 B is the best answer because it states the proper rule and is consistent with the facts in the fact pattern. Third party safety can make sex a BFOQ, where that safety is central to the essence of the employer's business, and some courts have held that privacy interests, at least when they are linked with safety concerns, in certain narrow circumstances can make sex a BFOQ. *See Healey v. Southwood Psychiatric Hosp.*, 78 F.3d 128 (3d Cir. 1996). Sex will only be a BFOQ if being one sex interferes with the ability to do the job. People of all sexes can perform massages. Moreover, this fact pattern does not link sex to same-sex preferences or sex-segregated spaces, which is generally where courts have recognized a privacy-based, sex BFOQ. This is a more ordinary kind of sex preference based on stereotypes about men and women.

A is not the best answer. The question is asked about the private sector, so the Constitution does not apply.

C is not correct because the Supreme Court has never directly held that privacy can make sex a BFOQ, it does not always do so, and C reflects the wrong rule. It is not that *privacy* is a BFOQ, privacy must make *sex* a BFOQ.

D is not correct. The chain is using sex as a hiring criterion. It is irrelevant that its purpose in using sex serves some additional, further purpose.

4.4 C is the best answer. This fact pattern is the core fact pattern in *UAW v. Johnson Controls*, 499 U.S. 187 (1991), where the Court held that a sex-based fetal protection policy was disparate treatment and that the policy could not be justified as a BFOQ because sex was unrelated to the ability to make batteries, and safety to fetuses was not central to the employer's business, which was to make batteries.

A is not the correct rule. Safety of employees themselves does not make sex a BFOQ. Allowing that would allow employers to engage in all kinds of paternalistic sexism. If safety is important (and it is), it is important for everyone, not just members of one sex.

B is the correct rule, in part, but it is not complete. Safety of third parties will make sex a BFOQ only where the safety of those third parties is part of the essence of the business of the employer. Even if fetuses could be third parties, this employer's business is to make batteries, not to protect fetuses.

D is not the best answer. It is true that the workers protected by the policy—all women of childbearing age—was overbroad in the sense that the policy didn't account for women who could not become pregnant but who were within the general parameters of what is considered childbearing age. But that is not the test for when sex will be a BFOQ.

**4.5** C is the best answer. Although the Supreme Court has never explicitly recognized it, there is a general consensus that "authenticity" can make sex a BFOQ, and the EEOC's regulations recognize that. 29 C.F.R. § 1604.2(a)(2). Where a product is marketed to a particular sex, and selling to that sex is the essence of the employer's business, having members of that sex wear the clothes to show how they would be worn by customers may make sex a BFOQ. This is an analogy to the example used in EEOC regulations of sex being a BFOQ for an actor or actress as a matter of authenticity. 29 C.F.R. § 1604.2(a)(2).

A is not the best answer. It is true that people of all sexes may be photogenic, but modelling clothing for sale to a particular customer base can require more than simply being photogenic.

B is not the best answer. It is true that people of all genders wear clothes, but the employer here is designing a product for and targeting a sex-based customer base. Tailoring products to the desires of a particular customer base does not violate Title VII even when the categories used are race, sex, religion, etc.

D is not the best answer because Title VII doesn't exclude any profession from coverage.

**4.6** This question inevitably gets the most discussion in my class. On the one hand, Hooters is a restaurant, and its business is to sell food. Serving that food can be done just as well by a person of any sex or gender. At the same time, Hooters is marketing itself as a particular kind of environment, where sexual titillation, primarily of straight men, is part of the environment. Waitstaff is not just female, but the appearance standards are very strict toward a certain aesthetic of beauty, and the uniform required is scanty and somewhat sexually provocative. It seems that Hooters is limiting servers to one sex because of customer preference for who should serve food at a restaurant, which we know can't make sex a bona fide occupational question. Hooters' best argument is that it is not simply selling food, but that it is selling a sexualized experience to people attracted to women. That is an attempt to frame the essence of the business in a way that makes sex, and sexuality, a core part. It is not clear that the EEOC would accept this framing or that courts would. The EEOC has challenged Hooters a number of times, and cases have been brought, but those cases have always settled.

**4.7** A is the best answer because even though not all women have uteruses, and some men also have uteruses, having a uterus is a requirement to be a gestational surrogate, and the vast proportion of those with uteruses are women.

B is incorrect because there is nothing about sex that enables a person to use or sell cosmetics.

C is not the best answer. It describes a situation where the Supreme Court did recognize that sex could be a BFOQ in certain narrow circumstances, but it is still less likely a BFOQ than A.

D is not the best answer. Even though professional football is a "men's" sport, for the most part in the U.S. (there are more men's teams), there is nothing specific and sex-linked to the ability to play football. In fact, there are women's teams, and women have played on professional men's teams.

# Conduct-Based Disparate Treatment: Retaliation

5.1 B is the best answer. The reason given by the employer for firing Jack was his testimony at a trial brought to enforce Title VII. The proceedings clause of Title VII's anti-retaliation provision offers extremely broad protection. It provides that an employer cannot discriminate against any person "because he has made a charge, testified, assisted, or participated in any manner in an investigation, proceeding, or hearing." under Title VII. The fact that the employer won the discrimination case is irrelevant, as is the fact that Jack's testimony sided with his employer and served its interest. Additionally, disruption is no defense to a retaliation claim.

A is not the best answer because the fact pattern does not suggest that the reason Jack was terminated was because he was male.

C is not the best answer because even though it is true that an employer has a legitimate interest in preventing sexual harassment, that is not the reason given for why Jack was fired. It was the fact of his testimony that the employer objected to.

D is not the best answer because this is a penalty for participation, not opposition, and the scope of protection of the participation clause is extremely broad.

5.2 A is the best answer. The fact pattern mirrors the facts of *Crawford v. Metropolitan Government of Nashville*, 555 U.S. 271 (2009), where the Court held that opposition conduct need not take any particular overt form to be protected. There, the plaintiff reported her own harassment by an employee under investigation for harassing a different employee. The plaintiff had not come forward to report the harassment herself but was simply a witness who reported her harassment when asked. The Court held that she clearly opposed that harassment, and so could not be terminated for reporting it in the interview. She was not required to first, voluntarily report to be protected or to demonstrate opposition to the harassing conduct.

B is not the best answer. Before the lower courts, the plaintiff in *Crawford* did argue that an employer's internal investigation counts as a proceeding protected by the proceedings clause, but the Court did not decide that issue, so it is not clear that the plaintiff's conduct would be protected by the proceedings clause.

C is not correct because the Court rejected this argument in *Crawford*. Opposition conduct will be protected as long as it opposes discrimination. The form of that opposition does not require a particular kind of voluntary expression.

**D** is not correct. A third-party retaliation claim would be where the employer terminated someone else as punishment to Aron. That is not the fact pattern here, where Aron was the one penalized. Also, third-party retaliation is actionable in certain circumstances.

5.3 **C** is the best answer. An employer retaliates against an employee under Title VII if it takes an adverse employment action against the employee for conduct protected under the statute (opposition or participation in proceedings). The retaliation provision describes the prohibited employer action using the term "discriminate," similar to the definition of disparate treatment, but does not limit that to discrimination in "compensation, terms, conditions, or privileges of employment" the way that the disparate treatment provision does. Accordingly, employer conduct will be an adverse employment action for purposes of retaliation when it is material. And it will be material when it would deter a reasonable employee from taking action. *Burlington Northern & Santa Fe Railway Co. v. White*, 548 U.S. 53 (2006). Answer C provides the correct rule, and is consistent with the facts. It is unlikely that removal from a fun activity would be enough to deter a reasonable employee from acting.

**A** is not the best answer because it does not state the correct rule. Under the opposition clause, it is not enough that the employee truly believes that what they oppose would violate Title VII. That belief must at least be reasonable also. In addition, the statement doesn't cover the complete rule. Even if this is a reasonable belief that the pay gap would violate Title VII, there is no retaliation unless the plaintiff suffers a material adverse employment action.

**B** is not a correct statement of the rule for when a consequence to the employee will constitute an adverse employment action. A negative change must be material.

**D** is not a correct statement of the rule for adverse employment actions under the retaliation provision of Title VII. That provision does not have the qualifying language that appears in the answer (a term or condition of employment), and that language is not complete even if what were at issue were disparate treatment.

5.4 **D** is the best answer because it provides a defense to any retaliation claim under Title VII, and it is consistent with the facts. The retaliation protections of Title VII prevent disparate treatment. An employer may not take action because of protected conduct, but the only conduct protected is opposition conduct or participation conduct. The conduct the employer wants to terminate Sara for is not for opposing discrimination (she didn't—she engaged in discrimination), nor is it the act of testifying in the proceedings. Instead, the conduct the employer is targeting is the discrimination and cover up, conduct penalized by Title VII, not protected by it.

**A** is not a good answer because the facts clearly say that Sara's participation was not the reason the employer wanted to act. Participation conduct does not create a blanket protection for employees, preventing their discharge for reasons unrelated to that participation.

Likewise, **B** and **C** are not good answers because the testimony isn't the reason for the proposed adverse action.

5.5 **B** is the best answer. Carl and Dave wore the masks to protest what they believed to be racially discriminatory action, and that belief was likely reasonable, since other divisive messages and statements related to ethnicity or race were allowed. This is protected opposition conduct. Adam and Ben's conduct was not protected opposition conduct, though, because it appeared that they were objecting to societal discrimination, rather than discrimination at Organics. The Court in *McDonnell Douglas v. Green*, 411 U.S. 792 (1973), held that Title VII's retaliation provisions only protect opposition to discrimination by a person's own employer, and not discrimination outside of that particular workplace. The discharge of Adam and Ben might have violated Title VII's prohibition on race discrimination, but it did not violate the retaliation provision.

**A** is not correct because Adam and Ben's conduct was probably not protected opposition conduct.

**C** is not correct because an employee need only oppose discrimination by the employer. They need not also have experienced discrimination.

**D** is not correct because speech that might be viewed as political will be protected by Title VII if that speech opposes discrimination by that employer.

5.6 **D** is the best answer. Even though Evan was the one who engaged in the protected conduct, a third-party who experienced an adverse employment action because of that protected conduct can bring a Title VII retaliation claim as long as that third-party's relationship with the person who engaged in the protected conduct is close enough. The materiality test, or question of whether the employer action would deter a reasonable employee from taking the protected action, is how to evaluate which relationships will give rise to a third-party retaliation claim.

**A** is not correct because, even if Frankie did not engage in protected conduct, his relationship with Evan might allow him to bring a third-party retaliation claim.

**B** is not correct because coworkers might have a close enough relationship to allow for a third-party retaliation claim.

**C** is not correct because that is not the test for a third-party retaliation claim or for any other retaliation claim.

5.7 **A** is the best answer. Mixed motive claims are not available in retaliation cases, so the fact that the employer had non-retaliatory motives likely means Glen would be unable to prove that retaliation was a but-for reason for her termination.

**B** is incorrect because it states a defense that is available only where mixed motive cases can be brought.

**C** is incorrect because it states the rule for mixed motive cases, and those are not cognizable for retaliation claims.

**D** is incorrect because it is not relevant in a retaliation case involving the proceedings clause.

# Systemic Disparate Treatment

6.1 **B is the best answer.** To state a prima facie case for a pattern and practice or systemic disparate treatment case through circumstantial evidence, a plaintiff must provide (1) statistical evidence showing a substantial disparity between those in the position at issue and those in the relevant labor pool plus (2) evidence of individual instances of disparate treatment. *International Brotherhood of Teamsters v. United States*, 431 U.S. 329 (1977); *Hazelwood School District v. United States*, 433 U.S. 299 (1977); *Wal-Mart Stores, Inc. v. Dukes*, 564 U.S. 338 (2011). This is a prima face in the usual sense of that term, not in the sense used in *McDonnell Douglas*. So proving this means that the plaintiff wins unless the defendant can prove an affirmative defense. B states the rule and is consistent with the facts, which indicate a substantial statistical disparity and individual instances of race-based disparate treatment.

**A is not the best answer** because it is not responsive to the facts. The statement is true, "pattern and practice" cases are governed by a different provision within Title VII than the usual enforcement provision, but systemic disparate treatment cases can be brought by individuals or the EEOC under section 706 (42 U.S.C. § 2000e-5), which is the "usual" provision, and "pattern and practice" cases can be brought by the EEOC under section 707 (42 U.S.C. § 2000e-6). Regardless, this fact is essentially irrelevant.

**C is not correct** because a systemic disparate treatment case can be proven through either direct or circumstantial evidence, just like individual disparate treatment.

**D is not correct** because the systemic disparate treatment case does not work like the *McDonnell Douglas* proof structure, and pretext is not a separate inquiry.

6.2 If the EEOC proves that an employer has engaged in a pattern and practice of discrimination, there are essentially two defenses. The employer can prove that the protected class is a BFOQ for the position in question, if the case involves sex, national origin, religion, or age. Alternatively, for any individual who was allegedly discriminated against, the defendant can avoid liability by proving that for this individual, the same result would have happened without considering their protected class. This latter, individual defense is available in race cases, also.

**6.3** **D** is the best answer. To prove a systemic disparate treatment or pattern and practice case, the plaintiff has to show a substantial disparity between those in the position and those in the labor pool, and some anecdotal instances of disparate treatment. The statistics alone may create an inference that discrimination is driving the disparity if the disparity is big enough. And an employer can rebut the plaintiff's evidence in a number of ways. It can attach the statistical evidence, or it can offer a different explanation for what is driving the disparity. Here, the fact that the employer was attempting to recruit women to the higher paying positions and the survey about job satisfaction might persuade a court that discrimination was not driving the disparity, but instead, the interests of applicants themselves. This "lack of interest defense" is controversial, but was accepted by the Seventh Circuit in *EEOC v. Sears, Robuck & Co.*, 839 F.2d 302 (7th Cir. 1988).

**A** is not the best answer because it is addressed at one, rarely used type of statistical evidence—regression analysis—used primarily in pay cases to help reject as many variables as possible to show that sex-based pay differentials are most likely caused by sex. That does not appear to be necessary here where the focus is on the type of jobs women and men do.

**B** is incorrect because business necessity is not a defense to a systemic disparate treatment case.

**C** is not correct because there is nothing about sex that makes one sex better at selling items that members of all sexes use.

**6.4** **A** is the best answer. Generally speaking, unless the statistical analysis shows such a disparity that it is nearly certain to create a strong inference of discrimination, like the "inexorable zero" in *Teamsters v. United States*, 431 U.S. 324 (1977), a plaintiff must also provide enough support through individual instances of disparate treatment to support the inference that discrimination motivated all of the decisions made. *Wal-Mart Stores, Inc. v. Dukes*, 564 U.S. 338 (2011). Six is almost certainly not enough to show that thousands of decisions were motivated by sex.

**B** is not correct because the "stray comments" doctrine means something else and has no applicability here. Comments are "stray" if they are so far removed from the decisionmaking process that they cannot bolster an inference about motive. Here, the comments were made by individual decisionmakers and so were not stray.

**C** is not correct because it does not do anything to negate the possibility that decisionmakers are making sex-based decisions.

**D** is not correct because there is no evidence that would support a lack of interest defense.

Topic 7 Answers

# Disparate Impact

7.1 C is the best answer. Even though disparate impact cases often involve a challenge to the effect of an objective qualification, like a credential or a test, that need not always be the case. Disparate impact is a framework that provides a way for employees to remove "built in headwinds" without having to prove that those headwinds were adopted for the purpose of excluding members of the protected class. The fact pattern here is nearly identical to that in *Watson v. Fort Worth Bank & Trust*, 487 U.S. 977 (1988), where the Court held that a plaintiff could challenge a wholly subjective decisionmaking process using the disparate impact framework.

A is not correct because disparate impact claims are not limited to situations where a test or credential caused a discriminatory effect.

B is not the best answer because the number of promotion decisions in the fact pattern is not necessarily the only evidence to be used to show a disparate impact, and it may be enough. There are challenges an employer can make to statistical analyses that rely on too small a sample size, but those are factual questions that cannot be resolved at the motion to dismiss stage.

D is not the best answer because it does not accurately state any rule. Wholly subjective decisionmaking processes may be infected by explicit or implicit bias, but the plaintiff has to prove that in each case.

7.2 In *Griggs v. Duke Power Co.*, 401 U.S. 424 (1971), the diploma requirement and the tests were not job related because people without them had performed just as well as people with them. There was no correlation between these requirements and success on the job.

7.3 Justice White dissented in *Dothard v. Rawlinson*, 433 U.S. 321, 347 (1977), because he did not believe that the general population made up the appropriate labor pool for the prison guard position. He would have defined the labor pool as including only those applying or interested in being prison guards. Specifically, he wrote,

> I am unwilling to believe that the percentage of women applying or interested in applying for jobs as prison guards in Alabama approximates the percentage of women either in the national or state population. A plaintiff could, of course, show that the composition of the applicant pool was distorted by the exclusion of nonapplicants

> who did not apply because of the allegedly discriminatory job requirement. But no such showing was made or even attempted here; and although I do not know what the actual fact is, I am not now convinced that a large percentage of the actual women applicants, or of those who are seriously interested in applying, for prison guard positions would fail to satisfy the height and weight requirements.

*Id.* at 348.

**7.4** Neither of these statistics compared the right groups—the demographics of those effected by the employment practice must be compared to the demographics of the relevant labor pool. If 81% of the NYCTA employees on methadone were Black or Hispanic, then it would not be a disparity at all that 81% of those referred to the medical director for suspected violation of the narcotics rule reflected these demographics. And even though, in the general population of the city, 63% of methadone users were Black or Hispanic, it was not clear how many of those worked for or wanted to work for the NYCTA. In other words, we can't measure the disparity caused by the narcotic rule by comparing 81% of referrals to the 63% of the general population because it is not clear that the labor pool had the same demographics as the general population.

**7.5** Justice White would have found the requisite comparison to have been shown. The plaintiffs showed that 63% of those who use methadone in the city were Black or Hispanic, although the population of the city as a whole was only 20% Black or Hispanic. So Black or Hispanic people were three times more likely to be excluded by the narcotics rule than a white person would be. This was enough, in his view, to show that the operation of the rule excluded Black and Hispanic people, disproportionately.

**7.6** Applicant pool data looks at the group who could apply, while applicant flow data looks at the passage rate of actual applicants.

**7.7** The short answer is, no. 50% of white test takers (25 ÷ 50 = .5) and 48% of Black test takers (12 ÷ 25 = .48) passed. Black test takers passed at nearly the same rate as white test takers (96%, 48 ÷ 50 = .96).

**7.8** *Calculate the rates of promotion for Black applicants (from application to promotion) and white applicants, and then compare the success rates of black to white applicants.*

To figure passage rate, divide the number of those promoted by the number of applicants and multiply by 100 to get the percentage. The percentage of white applicants promoted (overall) was 13.5% (35/259 = .135, *100 = 13.5). The percentage of Black applicants who were successfully promoted was 22.9% (11/48 = .229, *100 = 22.9).

*Calculate the rates of test passage for Black applicants and white applicants and compare the success rates of black to white applicants.*

To figure test passage rate, divide the number of those who passed by the number of those who took the test and multiply by 100 to get the percentage. Black test takers passed at a 54.2% rate (26/48 = .5416, *100 = 54.2). White test takers passed at a 79.5% rate (206/259 = .795, *100 = 79.5)

*Do either of these show a disparate impact on the basis of race? What were the arguments made about what calculation mattered?*

Compare the success rates of Black to white applicants. White applicants had the lower passage rate, so divide that rate by the rate of Black applicants. White applicants were promoted at about 59% the rate of Black applicants (13.5/22.0 = .5895, *100 = 59). This does not show a disparate impact against Black applicants, and may show a disparate impact against white applicants, since a rate difference of 59% is well below the 80% threshold that shows a presumptive disparate impact.

Compare the test passage rates of Black to white applicants. Here, Black test passage rates were lower than white test passage rates. Black applicants passed the test at about 68% of the rate that white applicants passed (54.2/79.5 = .682, *100 = 68). This shows a disparate impact on the basis of race for Black applicants because a rate difference of 68% is well below the 80% threshold that shows a presumptive disparate impact.

The plaintiffs, Black applicants, argued that because the test created a disparate racial impact, that the process violated Title VII. The employer argued that because the final promotion results showed no adverse impact on Black applicants that the process did not violate Title VII. This is the so-called "bottom line" defense.

7.9 C is the best answer. The word-of-mouth recruitment strategy has clearly led to a disparity between those hired and those in the eligible labor pool, which is the general population of the neighborhood since these are not skilled positions. If that method of recruitment cannot satisfy the business necessity test, then it will violate Title VII.

A is not correct because the employment practice of word-of-mouth hiring is an employment practice that can be pointed to as causing the disparity. It may not be neutral in the sense that there is a possibility the owners chose this method of hiring because they hoped it would result in a pool of candidates that was mostly Asian. But the plaintiff in a disparate impact suit doesn't have to prove that an employment practice is neutral, just that it causes a disparity.

B is not correct because the applicant pool is not the proper measure of the labor pool where there are no facts to suggest that the job requires special skills or is not generally desirable.

**D** is not correct because a disparity alone does not violate Title VII. Only when that disparity cannot be justified as a business necessity will it do so.

**7.10** **A** is the best answer. The hiring process seems to have created a disparate impact on the basis of race. 30% of Asian applicants were hired, about 27% of white applicants were hired and 0% of Black or Latino applicants were hired. The passage rate of Black and Latino applicants is clearly less than 80% of the rate of Asian applicants, and so there is a presumptive disparate impact. At the motion to dismiss stage, the only question is whether the plaintiffs can make a prima facie case of a disparate impact, and they can by alleging that the hiring process caused this disparity.

**B** is not the best answer because it frames the issue as disparate treatment. That is not necessary to withstand a motion to dismiss a disparate impact claim.

**C** is not the best answer because, even though plaintiffs have to point to the particular employment practice that causes the disparity, where the employer's processes cannot be separated for analysis, the plaintiff can point to that process as a whole as the cause. Here, it's not possible to separate the two parts of the hiring process because they are not separately scored.

**D** is not correct because Title VII protects individuals from discrimination. It is irrelevant that other people may not have been discriminated against based on race if the plaintiffs were. In other words, good treatment of one racial group is not a defense to a disparate impact claim.

# Defenses to Disparate Impact

8.1 **False.** If any step in the hiring process causes a disparate impact, it will violate Title VII unless that step is job related and consistent with business necessity. In other words, there is no "bottom line" defense to a disparate impact case.

8.2 C is the best answer. The Court held in *Griggs* that intent to treat members of a protected class differently was not required for a Title VII violation. Employment practices that had effects on a protected class would also violate Title VII unless those practices were job related and consistent with business necessity. A practice is job related when it predicts success at job performance, and it is consistent with business necessity when it measures the minimum qualifications for the job in question.

A is not the best answer because the district court had found that the employer had not adopted the employment practices with the purpose of keeping Black employees in the lowest paying positions, and the Court was bound by that factual finding. Moreover, the Court found intent was not relevant and that disparate effects could give rise to liability.

B is not the best answer because having a test professionally developed for this workplace is neither necessary nor sufficient to make that test job related and consistent with a business necessity. It is possible for tests adopted from other contexts to satisfy this standard, and it is possible for a professionally developed test for this workplace to fail it.

D is not the best answer because the settled expectations of the workers are irrelevant as a defense, although they, at times, may explain policy reasons behind what rule to adopt in interpreting Title VII.

8.3 A is the best answer. There is an actionable disparate impact case here, but the practice that causes the disparate impact appears to satisfy the business necessity test, and so the defendant will ultimately be successful. The hiring process has two steps, and if either one creates a disparate impact, that step will have to be job related and consistent with a business necessity. The first step, the test, creates a disparate impact because women pass at only 50% of the rate at which men pass (40/80 = .5, *100 = 50). 50% is below 80%, so the test creates a presumptive disparate impact. The test appears to be valid, though. It not only has content that is job related and necessary, but performance on the test appears to be correlated with better performance on the job as measured by performance reviews. Thus, it is likely not a violation of Title VII.

**B** is not a good answer because the quoted material leaves out important language. A professionally developed test will not violate Title VII so long as it is not used to discriminate. The Court has interpreted this language to mean that as long as a professionally developed test is valid—predicts success on the job—it will be job related and consistent with business necessity, and thus not used to discriminate.

**C** is not the best answer because it only contains the first part of the rule. It is true that the test creates a disparate impact, but a disparate impact violates Title VII only if it is not job related and consistent with business necessity.

**D** is not correct. An employer does not engage in disparate treatment by using a practice that has a disparate impact even when it knows about that impact. Only where the employer chooses the test because of that impact (as a way to intentionally discriminate) will the employer's action be disparate treatment.

**8.4** **B** is the best answer. To determine whether an employment practice causes a disparate impact, the demographics of the group with the desired position have to be compared to the demographics of the group that could be in the desired position. In *Wards Cove v. Atonio*, 490 U.S. 642 (1989), the lower court compared cannery jobs to non-cannery jobs, but the people in the cannery jobs did not make up the labor pool for the non-cannery jobs. Cannery jobs required mostly "unskilled" labor (physical tasks that could be performed without formal training), while non-cannery jobs involved "skilled" labor (tasks that traditionally are done by those with formal training and education). Those in cannery jobs lacked the qualifications for most non-cannery jobs.

**A** is not the best answer because statistical proof alone does make out a prima facie case of disparate impact discrimination.

**C** is not the best answer because subjective employment criteria can be challenged on a disparate impact theory. *Watson v. Ft. Worth Bank & Trust*, 487 U.S. 977 (1988).

**D** is not the best answer because the Court never reached this issue. It didn't get past the prima facie case of disparate impact.

**8.5** **C** is the best answer. This fact pattern is very similar to the fact pattern in *Griggs v. Duke Power Co.*, where the employer instituted a high school degree requirement on the theory that it would produce a better class of worker. Unless that credential can be shown to be job related and consistent with business necessity, a disparate impact created by that credential will violate Title VII.

**A** is not correct because there is no minimum number of charges that would need to be filed before the EEOC can bring an action. In fact, an EEOC Commissioner can bring an action on their own.

**B** is not correct because, if the employment practice of requiring a bachelor's degree results in a disparate impact, Title VII can redress use of that employment practice.

**D** is not correct because it is framed in terms of a bona fide occupational qualification, which is a defense to disparate treatment, while this fact pattern suggests that disparate impact is the appropriate framework.

# Harassment

9.1 D is the best answer. In order to state a claim for hostile environment sex harassment, i.e., a situation where enduring the harassment is a condition of not suffering a tangible employment action, a plaintiff has to prove, among other things, that the conduct was so severe or pervasive that a reasonable person would perceive it to have created an abusive working environment. Conduct is severe when it is humiliating, offensive, threatening, or intimidating. Conduct is pervasive when it happens frequently, over time or is otherwise widespread. The conduct doesn't have to be both, but they do operate on a sliding scale. The more severe, the less pervasive conduct must be to be actionable and vice versa. Although hearing a racial epithet is pretty severe, it happened once. Some courts have held that a single instance of being called a racial epithet may be severe enough to create a hostile work environment such that there is no need to consider multiple events. But simply hearing a racial epithet is less severe, such that a single instance may not be enough to make the environment actionable.

A is not correct because harassment is simply a form of discrimination and will be unlawful based on any of the classes protected by Title VII or other anti-discrimination law.

B is not correct because harassment can make an environment so hostile that the environment becomes an adverse term, condition, or privilege of employment.

C is incorrect. Although harassing conduct may at times be outside the scope of a supervisor's job duties, an employer can be liable for the supervisor's actions if it fails to prevent or remedy harassment that it knows or should know about.

9.2 B is the best answer. In order to be severe, conduct must be humiliating, offensive, threatening, or intimidating. And while these comments are clearly upsetting to Glen, since they bring an action, a reasonable person would probably not experience even a year's worth of daily comments that are just generally about a shapely body as creating an abusive workplace.

A is not correct. The "stray comments" doctrine generally provides that comments by non-decisionmakers or co-workers cannot be used to prove that the decisionmaker was motivated by a person's protected class in most situations. There are enough facts here by the main actor to suggest that sex was the reason for the harassment; and these comments are what make up the alleged harassment. They are not stray.

**C** is not correct because a hostile environment can give rise to an actionable claim. A constructive discharge is not necessary

**D** is not correct because sex-based harassment does not have to include such a demand. That would be a form of tangible employment action harassment, in common terms that are not a legal term of art, quid pro quo harassment, which is also actionable. But hostile environment harassment need not include that.

**9.3** **A** is the best answer. When a supervisor conditions a tangible employment action on submission to sexual advances, that constitutes actionable harassment. It doesn't matter whether the person complies and experiences the tangible employment action, or fails to comply and experiences the consequences of the opposite tangible employment action. And an employer is vicariously liable for this tangible employment action.

**B** is not the best answer because, while sexual advances can create a hostile environment, where there is a tangible employment action connected, that governs the analysis.

**C** is incorrect because the promotion was a tangible employment action. The injury was that Mel had to submit to a sexual advance to get the promotion while someone of a different sex would not have to.

**D** is incorrect because Mel suffered a tangible employment action, which makes the employer automatically vicariously liable. Only in hostile environment cases will an unreasonable failure to follow the employer's harassment policy and report the advance potentially be a defense.

**9.4** **A** is the best answer because it accurately states the rule for cases that involve constructive discharge. Where an employee is constructively discharged, an employer, generally, should be held to the same standards as if the employee was discharged outright. At the same time, under agency principles, where the hostile environment that led to an employee leaving is caused by a supervisor, an employer is not vicariously liable, but only liable for failing to prevent or remedy harassment it should have known about. The employer in this situation is presumed to be liable, but has an affirmative defense that the employee unreasonably failed to take advantage of opportunities to prevent or remedy the harassment. A supervisor is someone with the power to take tangible employment actions against the employee. So, the constructive discharge rule, to harmonize all of these rules, provides that if a constructive discharge is precipitated by some "official action" taken by a supervisor, then it will be treated like a tangible employment action case, and the affirmative defense will not be available. Conversely if the constructive discharge was not precipitated by some "official action," then it is an ordinary hostile environment case, and the employer will have the affirmative defense.

**B** is not correct because a person who quits as a result of an environment that would make a reasonable employee feel they had no other choice is considered to have been constructively discharged, which is treated the same as an explicit discharge.

C is not correct because employers are not always liable for the conduct of supervisors under agency principles.

D is not the best answer because, if Emma can prove the constructive discharge claim that she alleges and her leaving was precipitated by an official act, as answer A states, then the employer will not have the affirmative defense.

**9.5** If Emma's supervisor lacked the power to hire or fire her, then they were not really a supervisor for purposes of Title VII, but instead were a coworker. To hold an employer liable for coworker harassment, in addition to the other elements of a hostile environment claim, the employee has to prove that the employer was negligent—that it failed to prevent or remedy harassment that it knew or should have known about.

**9.6** C is the best answer. The fact pattern describes potential hostile environment racial harassment by a supervisor. An employer will be vicariously liable for harassment by a supervisor in these circumstances if it fails to prevent or remedy that harassment. However, the employer acted immediately to move the supervisor, which remedied the harassment. Therefore, the employer is not liable.

A is not the best answer because prompt reporting by an employee is only one part of the analysis. If the employer acts properly to remedy the harassment, then there will be no liability.

B is not the best answer because it is not complete. Even though employers are vicariously liable for the conduct that supervisors engage in, they are only liable if they fail to take prompt remedial action.

D is not the best answer because, even without a tangible employment action, Frank might have a hostile environment claim.

**9.7** B is the best answer. If Frank's supervisor does not have the power to fire him, then that supervisor is actually a coworker, for purposes of employer liability, and in coworker hostile environment harassment cases, the employee has to prove that the employer was negligent in order for the employer to be liable. An employer is negligent if it knew or should have known about harassment but failed to prevent or remedy it.

A is not the best answer because it is not complete. It is true that if Frank never reported the harassment, it's more likely the company would not have known about it and would not be expected to have known. But reporting is not the only way that a company might be held to the standard of "knows or should know" about the harassment. If the harassment is very flagrant, and lots of employees and other supervisors witness it, that could suffice.

C is not correct because it frames the issue as an affirmative defense for the employer. For coworker harassment, the employee must prove employer negligence. It is not the employer's affirmative defense to prove it was not negligent. That is flipped in a case where the hostile environment is created by a true supervisor. In that instance, negligence is presumed, but the employer has an opportunity through its affirmative defense to prove it was not negligent.

D is not correct because it does not account for the entire burden that an employee bears in a coworker harassment case. A coworker hostile environment harassment case requires that the plaintiff prove that the employer was negligent.

**9.8** A is the best answer. For hostile environment harassment by a supervisor, an employer will have an affirmative defense that it acted promptly to prevent or remedy harassing behavior and the employee unreasonably failed to take advantage of preventative or corrective opportunities. An employee does not act unreasonably if reporting would be futile. Since reporting did not end the harassment in the fact pattern and in fact spread it, it seems reasonable to conclude that reporting would be futile.

B is not a good answer because Tortion can be liable for hostile environment harassment.

C is not correct because employees do not have to take advantage of an employer's processes if they exist. In fact, if taking advantage of those processes would be futile, an employee does not act unreasonably by failing to take advantage of them.

D is not the best answer because even though individuals are not liable under Title VII, the question asks about harassment, not retaliation. Moreover, the employer can be liable for conduct engaged in by coworkers.

**9.9** D is the best answer. It appears that Glen is abusive to people of multiple sexes, and the content and context of the harassment does not seem to implicate sex, race, color, national origin, or religion. Harassment is simply a form of discrimination, but it must be discrimination because of one of Title VII's protected classes to be actionable under that statute. Accordingly, it does not appear that Sue and Ted have a cause of action under that statute.

A is not correct, even though the conduct might meet the severe or pervasive standard. If it is not because of a class protected by Title VII, it is not actionable under the statute.

B is not correct because Ted may have suffered a tangible employment action, and the fact remains that the conduct must be because of a class protected by Title VII, or it is not actionable under the statute.

C is not correct because it is not the test for harassment or employer liability, necessarily. Additionally, assigning work and performing reviews is generally within the scope of a supervisor's duties.

Topic 10 **Answers**

# Focused Issues Related to Protected Classes: Race/Color

**10.1** This question of what race is can be a challenging one, in part because race is a social category, but one that at least on the surface has come to be linked with some physical characteristics like skin color, hair color and texture, and some facial features. Additionally, race is thought to be hereditary, in that a person inherits the race(s) of their parents to some extent.

**10.2** Race is a social construct in the sense that it is not genetic, and there is more biological variation among members of the same race than between races. The characteristics that assign people to a race are arbitrary. Why pick skin color and not left-handedness, for example? Additionally, people move in and out of racial categories over time.

The complication for anti-discrimination law is that if race is not physiological, then perhaps it is not immutable and does not deserve protection. But even as a social construct, race has persisted as a social category that produces inequality with intergenerational effects.

**10.3** B is the best answer because the language of § 1981 puts protection in terms of white citizens:

> All persons within the jurisdiction of the United States shall have the same right in every State and Territory to make and enforce contracts . . . as is enjoyed by white citizens . . . .

Title VII, by using the term "race," protects everyone who has a race, but the wording of § 1981 suggests that white people don't need legal protection from discrimination because they are at the top of the social hierarchy. The Court rejected that reading, but it was more plausible based on the language of § 1981 than it would be under Title VII.

A is not correct because whiteness is a race.

C is not correct because the employment relationship is considered contractual even if there is no explicit contract and even when it can be terminated at will.

**D** is not the best answer because, even though the plaintiffs committed theft, if the employer retained other employees who also committed theft, then theft was not a but-for reason for their termination and race might be. This analysis would be the same under Title VII and § 1981.

**10.4** **A** is the correct answer. In *Saint Francis College v. al-Khazraji*, 481 U.S. 604 (1987), the Supreme Court held that its role was to interpret the language used in § 1981 according to what the terms meant when the statute was passed in 1866. Accordingly, it looked to how race was defined in the mid-19th century.

**B** is not the best answer because the view of what race is has evolved over time, and the Court's role was to enforce its earlier meaning.

**C** is not the best answer because it does not conform to what race meant in 1866, even though it roughly conforms to a mid-to-late twentieth century view of race.

**D** is not the best answer because there really isn't a scientific definition of what constitutes race, and it's not really a genetic category.

**10.5** **C** is the best answer because it's the only answer that provides the correct rule that fits the fact pattern, which describes disparate impact. The shaving requirement clearly has a disparate impact on Black men, who, generally, can satisfy the requirement at 58% of the rate that white men can satisfy it. 50% of Black men can satisfy the requirement, but 85% of white men can. (100 - 15% with the condition = 85), and 50 is 58% of 85. But a disparate impact does not violate Title VII if the employment practice, here the shaving rule, is job related and consistent with business necessity.

Although it isn't as compelling as it could be, the employer does have some evidence that allowing salespeople with facial hair could make them less effective salespeople, resulting in a measurable drop in sales. The business necessity test does not necessarily require more than this simple correlation with performance. Even though this sounds suspiciously like customer preference, and you may remember that customer preference can't be a defense, that rule is linked to the BFOQ and a preference for a specific class. This isn't a situation where the employer is arguing that customers prefer white salespeople, instead, the employer is arguing that customers prefer clean shaven people of any race.

**A** is not the best answer because BFOQ is a defense to disparate treatment, and this is disparate impact. Additionally, the phrasing of what would be required for a BFOQ is incorrect. Shaving would have to make Claude's class a BFOQ. Lastly, race can never be a BFOQ.

**B** is not the best answer because it provides a test that has been adopted for sex specific grooming codes rather than the test applicable to disparate impact.

**D** is not the best answer because disparate impact liability does not require that the trait at issue be perfectly correlated with a single race. That would only matter if the plaintiff's argument was disparate treatment—that the ability to shave is itself race.

**10.6** C is the best answer. In *St. Francis College v. al-Khazraji*, 481 U.S. 604 (1987), the Court held that it had to look to what race meant at the time § 1981 was passed to determine what the term meant. Because the term mapped roughly onto modern concepts of national identity and ethnic heritage, Iraqi was a race for purposes of § 1981.

A is not the best answer because, even though today or in 1964 when Title VII passed, we might view race and national origin as separate categories, that was not the view when § 1981 was enacted, and regardless, there is significant overlap in the concepts even today.

B is not the best answer because, although the defendant argued that a person of Iraqi heritage today would be considered Caucasian, particularly if that person had very light colored skin, that fact is irrelevant to what race would have been considered to be in 1866 when § 1981 was enacted.

D is not the best answer because it focuses on the present. What Dr. al-Khazraji's race would be considered to be today is not relevant.

**10.7** A is the best answer. Rebecca is being penalized for her hair texture and its resulting appearance in its natural state, as it grows from her head. Hair texture is immutable, linked to race, even though people of all races can have many different types of hair. This question is tricky, because most cases considering whether grooming codes are racially discriminatory have found no disparate treatment. Those cases, however, considered whether prohibitions on protective hairstyles, like locs, braids, and twists, were race discrimination. It is generally recognized that penalizing Afros, the natural result of a particular hair texture, or hair the way it grows from one's head, would constitute race discrimination. *Jenkins v. Blue Cross Mutual Hospital Insurance, Inc.*, 538 F.2d 164, 168 (7th Cir. 1976) (en banc) (finding race discrimination where plaintiff was penalized for having an Afro); *Rogers v. American Airlines, Inc.*, 527 F. Supp. 229, 232 (S.D.N.Y. 1981) (distinguishing braids from Afros).

B is not the best answer because courts have generally held that employers can dictate matters of personal appearance, at least at work. This is a consequence of the at-will rule.

C is not the best answer because, although a hairstyle can be changed, and thus is not immutable, Afros are considered to be a natural consequence of hair texture, which is immutable.

D is not the best answer because a policy can be discriminatory even if it doesn't mention a protected class by focusing on something linked to one class, by being enforced differently based on class, or if it was adopted as a way to discriminate against a protected class.

**10.8** C is the best answer. Discriminating against a person because of the race of people they associate with is race discrimination under Title VII. And based on these facts, a reasonable jury could find that the information about the racial makeup of Cary's neighborhood and his spouse's race were what caused the company to fire him.

A is not correct because whiteness is a race protected by Title VII. Also, this claim was about discrimination on the basis of association with Black people.

**B** is not the best answer. Even where language is not explicit, a factfinder can interpret the whole context of a situation to make an inference, and the combination of the sudden change of heart upon learning information about the race of Cary's neighbors and spouse with the coded language could lead a reasonable factfinder to conclude that race was the reason for the termination.

**D** is not correct. If the allegations in the complaint do not state a plausible claim, then a motion to dismiss is proper.

**10.9** **B** is the best answer. Diana clearly terminated Elisha for changing her hairstyle, and that hairstyle is one culturally associated with Black people based on the immutable characteristic of hair texture. Additionally, Diana used a term often derogatorily used against Black people in referring to her hairstyle. Lastly, there is nothing unprofessional about a braided hairstyle. All of these facts could lead a reasonable jury to conclude that Diana was motivated by race in deciding to terminate Elisha.

**A** is not the best answer because, even if the grooming code did explicitly prohibit braids, that prohibition might violate Title VII. Moreover, Diana used a race-linked derogatory term, showing that she was motivated by race in applying whatever grooming code existed.

**C** is not the best answer because people of the same group can discriminate against each other. Additionally, some people downplay their marginalized identity at work to succeed, and may resent or punish other members of their group who don't do the same thing.

**D** is not the best answer because, even though hairstyles are mutable, that doesn't negate the fact that Diana seems to be motivated by the fact that the hairstyle is linked with Blackness in making her decision.

**10.10** **D** is the best answer. Despite the fact that color discrimination is not uncommon, because our concept of race is linked with skin color, it is rare to see a color discrimination case separate from a race discrimination case. But this fact pattern presents one. Here, skin color appears to be the criterion the employer is using to decide who gets jobs that are visible to customers and who gets jobs that are not. And that distinction comes with a pay difference, at least for Darius's position.

**A** is not correct because Title VII prohibits color discrimination explicitly. Even though there is significant overlap between race and color, given how we define that social category in the U.S., Title VII allows for them to be differently considered, and they are separate vectors of marginalization. Darker skinned people are often discriminated against in favor of lighter skinned people.

**B** is not correct because Darius's compensation is affected by his position, and that is explicitly defined as a potential unfair employment practice by Title VII.

**C** is not correct because information about the demographics of the local labor pool are not required to show what the employer's motive was. That kind of information can be helpful, but it is not necessary.

**10.11** This isn't a traditional kind of multiple choice question, because it doesn't exactly test a legal question, strictly speaking. It's a great way to think about counseling clients in the workplace, though, and about one's own interactions with people. **A** is quite clearly the best answer here. The decisions that employees make about their own lives, and their families, are none of an employer's business. The other options invite a person to engage in patronizing stereotyping and perpetuate other people's racism.

**B** is not as good as A because it reflects a mindset that it is the employee's job to act in ways that sidestep others' discriminatory motives. Also, what happens if the employee does see the article and either pays no attention or gets angry about the passive aggressive action? Does that set up the opportunity for the supervisor to treat this employee differently because of her race?

**C** is not a good answer because it suggests that the supervisor thinks there is something wrong with being Black.

**D** is not a good answer because, even though it is framed in benevolent terms, it still communicates that there is something wrong with being Black and that assimilation to whiteness is the better option.

# Focused Issues Related to Protected Classes: National Origin

11.1 **False.** Although national origin is closely linked to citizenship, for example, everyone born in the U.S. has U.S. citizenship, and fewer people born in other countries have U.S. citizenship, they are not identical enough to say that citizenship is national origin.

11.2 **True.** This may seem inconsistent with the prior answer, but language is not only closely linked to the place of one's birth, it is also linked with ethnic heritage and ancestry. As a result, the EEOC considers and courts have generally held that discrimination on the basis of language spoken may be disparate treatment on the basis of national origin in certain circumstances.

11.3 **Probably not.** Because part of the national character of the United States is that its members—those who are not from indigenous nations that existed when colonization began—are members of the ethnic group of their ancestors before those ancestors came or were brought to the U.S. Descendants of those brought forcefully to the U.S. as enslaved persons are often grouped together into a "racial" category rather than an ethnic category, since culture, language and even knowledge of one's ancestors was forcibly prevented.

Many people in the U.S., at least, don't tend to think of the shared U.S. cultural similarity as ethnic or inherited from one generation to the next. So, it is hard to say that there is such a thing as U.S. national origin. At the same time, many in the U.S. either cannot, because it is unknown, or do not identify with the nation of origin of their ancestors. So perhaps there is a unique U.S. national origin for some people who pass down their culture from one generation to the next.

11.4 C is the best answer. EEOC regulations state that a rule which requires that English be spoken at all times burdens an essential national origin characteristic, disadvantages employment opportunities on the basis of national origin, and may create a hostile environment, so will be presumed to violate Title VII and be "closely scrutinized." 29 C.F.R. § 1606.7(a). This is essentially an assumption that the adoption of the rule is motivated by national origin and is disparate treatment. Thus, it can only be justified if speaking English at all times (which is here the same as national origin) is a BFOQ.

Requiring English at only certain times or in certain places, on the other hand, is disparate impact, which must be justified by business necessity. 29 C.F.R. § 1606.7(b).

A is not the best answer because this conduct is so closely linked to national origin that it counts as national origin itself.

B is not correct because the question here is whether the policy itself violates Title VII. If it does, or if the policy is only applied based on the protected status of the person, then that will violate Title VII.

D is not the best answer because, while true, Title VII does not require employers to exercise good business sense.

**11.5** A is the best answer. The comments made by the manager expressed strong anti-Latino sentiments, suggesting that the reason for termination only two weeks later was linked to her national origin, or perhaps the fact that she was a pregnant Latina, an intersectional claim.

B is not correct because pregnant employees do not need to be accommodated under Title VII and do not have job security rights under it.

C is not correct. The manager's focus on "Mexicans" when Luisa is from Guatemala simply helps demonstrate that he was engaged in stereotypical biases about Latino workers in general.

D is not correct because at-will employees are protected from discrimination under Title VII.

**11.6** C is the best answer. The request to Anglicize Jie's name and the justification that he was too "ethnic" show that the interviewer was motivated by Jie's national origin. And even though Jie is a U.S. citizen, national origin is generally an ethnic concept that encompasses where a person's ancestors come from.

A is incorrect because national origin encompasses ethnicity as well as the nation in which a person is born

B is not correct because the interviewer did not base his decision on any objectionable behavior by Jie, but rather on his identity.

D is not correct because the identity of the clientele is irrelevant. Customer preference cannot make national origin a BFOQ.

**11.7** B is the best answer. The employer is discriminating against those with a U.S. nation of origin, which is national origin discrimination. He also seems to be using stereotypes about foreign born workers to justify that discrimination.

A is incorrect because companies are not required to prefer U.S. citizens.

C is not correct because, even though discrimination on the basis of citizenship doesn't always violate Title VII, that does not appear to be the kind of discrimination happening here. Rather, the employer appears to be literally distinguishing based on country of birth.

D is not correct because a decision can be discriminatory even if the employer doesn't always discriminate. Additionally, nation of origin is one of the meanings of national origin; it isn't only ethnic origin.

**11.8** D is the best answer. All of that context together suggests that national origin is the reason for the supervisor's harassment. That it might also be sex discrimination does not take away the national origin component; rather, this is an intersectional claim.

A is not correct because it is not the standard under Title VII, which protects individuals from discrimination. Moreover, the fact that only Latinas are targeted bolsters the conclusion that the reason for the harassment is their national origin. Comments about promiscuity are linked to many ethnic groups, but they often appear as a justification for sexualizing people in that group.

B is not the best answer. It is true that Fisheries, Inc. may have an affirmative defense for the harassment, but if the harassment is so open and well known, then it will likely not be able to satisfy the affirmative defense. Regardless of whether the harassment was reported, it may rise to the level where the employer should have known about it.

C is not correct because quid pro quo harassment, a term without as much legal significance as it once had, is not the kind of harassment described here.

## Topic 12 Answers

# Focused Issues Related to Protected Classes: Sex

12.1 Discussion or committee reports often help courts understand what Congress believed it was trying to address with its legislation, but sex does not have any real legislative history or legislative evidence to interpret for the original enactment of Title VII. It was added to the bill without any real debate, two days before the House voted on the Civil Rights Act of 1964 by a representative who opposed the Act.

12.2 The causes of the gender pay and achievement gaps are hotly debated. Some reasons for the gaps include labor market segregation, harassment, continued sex-based discrimination, fewer hours and time away from work for caregiving responsibilities. The U.S. does not have a robust social safety net to support worker health or families, and much of this responsibility falls to women in heterosexual families or single-head-of-household families. The causes of these reasons and whether government should play a role in changing them are also hotly debated.

12.3 A is the best answer. In *City of Los Angeles Department of Water & Power v. Manhart*, 435 U.S. 702 (1978), the Court held that employers could not rely on generalizations about protected classes to provide benefits, even when those generalizations were true in the aggregate. These are descriptive stereotypes—statistically true facts about a group. Title VII requires a focus on individuals, and individuals don't necessarily fit the stereotype. Plus, for pension benefits, it is impossible to know in advance who will or will not fit the stereotype.

B is not correct because the design of the program was to ensure that women as a group would get the same income from the employer instead of more than men.

C is not correct; it provides the argument made by the employer—its rationale for requiring women to pay more towards their pension—which was rejected by the Court.

D is not correct because it describes a real difference between men and women as groups, not individuals.

**12.4** **B** is the best answer. Jane was clearly qualified, and her appearance conformed to the grooming policy. The facts also demonstrate that the only reason Evelyn denied Jane the promotion was her appearance. And the comment Evelyn made about the "softball, tomboy look" of Jane reflects stereotypes about a woman appearing masculine.

A is incorrect because it does not appear that the dress code has sex-specific rules.

C is not correct because the manager appears to have only been upset by Jane's appearance because she was a woman. Why else use the term "tomboy"?

D is not correct because members of a protected class can discriminate against other members of their own class. Women can discriminate against women.

**12.5** C is the best answer because all of the elements for harassment liability are satisfied by this fact pattern. In order to be actionable, harassment must either result in a tangible employment action or include conduct that is so severe or pervasive that a reasonable person would find they create an abusive working environment. This conduct is severe. It is humiliating and intimidating and involves assault. It also appears to be relatively pervasive, since the name calling happens every day. The harassment appears to be because of sex, too. The terms used are gendered insults, and the physical assaults had sexual components. The sexuality of Blain, Carl, and Dean are irrelevant, since the content itself is focused on Blaine's sex. And the employer will be liable because it knows of the harassment and does not prevent or remedy it.

A is not correct because same sex harassment is discrimination under Title VII and was even before the Court decided *Bostock v. Clayton County*, 140 S. Ct. 1731 (2020).

B is not correct. The conduct described goes well beyond "horseplay," which suggests a joking, lighthearted, and mutual atmosphere.

D is not correct because the conduct is clearly because of sex because of the sex-linked content. Courts have often used sexuality and presumed desire as a shorthand way to conclude that conduct with sexual content is because of sex. But presumed desire is not the only way to make that inference, and it is unnecessary in this fact pattern.

**12.6** C is the best answer. Both men and women lacked restroom facilities outdoors, and so the lack of facilities is not disparate treatment. It was just easier based on their anatomy for most men to function without those facilities. Thus, the lack of outdoor facilities imposed a disparate impact.

A is not correct because there were no outdoor facilities for any sex.

B is not correct because the "effective" lack of women's bathrooms was a consequence of women's and men's differences.

D is not correct because it is not clear that the women needed more breaks than men, just facilities.

**12.7** **A** is the best answer. This question focuses on a challenging issue related to stereotypes. An employer can prefer the trait that is a stereotype as long as it prefers that trait in people of all sexes. Here, John isn't being penalized for acting a way that men are not supposed to act—it's not that but for his sex he wouldn't be penalized for being macho.

Although the question asks about disparate treatment, you might be worried about disparate impact, but **A** would also be correct there. Preferring that trait may cause a disparate impact if more women than men have it. But a disparate impact will violate Title VII only if it is not job related and consistent with business necessity. If being nurturing and cooperative (non-macho traits) are job related and necessary skills, the employer can require them even if doing so causes a disparate impact on men.

**B** is not correct because linking terms and conditions of work to conformance to stereotypes is a violation of Title VII even if that stereotype might be viewed as "positive." Plus, not all stereotypes of men are positive.

**C** is incorrect because it misstates the rule. Sex stereotyping does not automatically result in liability. It only results in liability when an employment action is linked to it.

**D** is incorrect because people can discriminate against members of their own group.

**12.8** **A** is the best answer. Although the Supreme Court has never decided a case involving sex-specific grooming codes, some circuit courts have held that sex specific grooming codes will only violate Title VII where they pose an undue burden on one sex. Here, sexualizing the information on women's name badges arguably creates a significantly more uncomfortable working environment for women.

**B** is not correct because it does not state the rule for sex-specific grooming codes.

**C** is not correct because, even though the information was sexualized and maybe embarrassing, it was not likely intimidating or humiliating, and so not as severe as something like an assault. It may make a sexualized environment pervasive, and so may result in hostile environment liability, but it is almost certainly not severe.

**D** is incorrect because it provides the rule for a BFOQ. That does not apply in the grooming code context.

**12.9** **B** is the best answer. Under Title VII, employers cannot discriminate on the basis of sex in the provision of benefits. Employers can provide benefits for recovery from birth to those recovering from birth and not to those who become parents in other ways, but that is not what this policy does. It provides leave for women who become parents or caregivers of children even when they do not need the leave to recover from birth. It also provides leave for longer than is generally thought necessary to recover from birth. Because the leave is not limited to recovery from birth, it must be provided on the same terms to everyone who becomes a parent.

**A** is not correct because pregnancy leave can be treated more favorably than other types of leave, as long as it is tied to pregnancy and birth. *California Federal Savings & Loan Association v. Guerra*, 479 U.S. 272 (1987).

**C** is not correct because the Pregnancy Discrimination Act's amendment to Title VII does not provide the only way that employer action can be sex discrimination.

**D** is not correct because the policy makes a distinction based on sex, not non-pregnancy.

**12.10** **A** is the best answer because it uses the language of Title VII's disparate treatment provision.

**B** is incorrect because it overstates the Court's holding in *Bostock v. Clayton County*, 140 S. Ct. 1731 (2020). In that case, the Court held that firing a person simply because they are transgender is sex discrimination under Title VII. However, the Court left open what other employer actions would constitute sex discrimination, and specifically left open the question of sex-segregated spaces.

**C** is incorrect because it does not state a rule applicable in this context. The undue burden standard applies only to sex specific grooming standards.

**D** is incorrect. No court has held that maintaining sex segregated facilities like restrooms and locker rooms are per se violations of Title VII.

**12.11** **D** is the best answer. This fact pattern presents a situation nearly identical to that at issue in *Bostock*, where the Court held that firing someone for being gay constituted sex discrimination under Title VII. But for Megan's sex, her marriage to a woman would not have caused her supervisor to fire her. The Court explicitly stated that saying you would take the same action against a man married to a man was no excuse—it was instead also sex discrimination.

**A** is not correct because, for both situations, but for their sex, their conduct would not have caused their termination. If, on the other hand, the supervisor would have fired Megan for marrying a man, then the supervisor would have been engaged in equal opportunity "discrimination."

**B** is not correct because Megan was engaged in conduct that her supervisor objected to only because of Megan's sex.

**C** is incorrect because Title VII does not protect the right to marry, and the fact pattern appears to take place in the private sector, not the public sector, so the Constitution would not apply.

**12.12** **A** is the best answer. Title VII requires that pregnant workers be treated the same as other workers in their ability or inability to work. The Supreme Court interpreted that in *Young v. United Parcel Service*, 575 U.S. 206 (2015), not to require that pregnancy receive "most favored nation" status. In other words, pregnancy need not be accommodated simply because one class of employees is accommodated. Instead, the Court used something of a balancing test that gets at whether employees are accommodated for multiple reasons and, if so, whether extending those reasons to pregnancy would create too much of a burden on the employer. Here, it sounds like only one group of employees is accommodated, which makes the balance less likely to require the employer to extend leave to pregnant employees, as well.

**B** is not correct because it's not a correct statement of any sort of analysis. Pregnancy itself may not be an impairment, but it can cause lots of impairments that must be accommodated under the ADA.

**C** is not correct because it is not a correct statement of the rule. The PDA requires only equal treatment, not accommodation of pregnancy.

**D** is not correct. The PDA does not require "most favored nation" status for pregnancy leave. In fact, leave for a single group is not likely to require leave for pregnant employees unless that single group includes a large number of employees.

**12.13** **B** is the best answer. Employees are allowed to engage in any activity consistent with the reason they require leave under the FMLA without forfeiting its protections. FMLA leave connected with a new child is provided to allow for bonding with that child and getting things organized at home. That is why it is provided to all parents regardless of who gave birth to the child and why it applies to foster placements. A vacation is entirely consistent with that bonding leave, and even a vacation away from the child might be if that vacation helps the caregiver have the emotional capacity to engage in the caregiving the FMLA protects.

**A** is not correct because the FMLA does not protect privacy in this way, and very few other laws would, either.

**C** is not correct because vacation is not necessarily inconsistent even with leave taken for medical reasons. For example, a vacation might be suggested by a healthcare professional to speed recovery where that vacation might reduce stress or allow for specialized care.

**D** is not correct because the leave provided by the FMLA is not limited to a person's own serious health needs.

**12.14** **C** is the best answer because lactation is a natural consequence of pregnancy and birth, and thus seems to fit the PDA's language defining sex as including (but not limited to) pregnancy, childbirth, or related medical conditions. The term "medical" does not need to have any sort of negative meaning, like a dysfunction. Although some courts early on gave "medical" a narrow and negative meaning, the more recent trend is to include lactation as protected.

**A** is not a good answer because, even if the ADA does not require an accommodation, Title VII might consider it sex discrimination if other employees are allowed breaks for other reasons. Additionally, it seems like the supervisor acted because of the fact of lactation rather than simply denying the accommodation.

**B** is not correct because "medical" need not imply some function that has gone wrong.

**D** is not correct because, even though the Affordable Care Act added a provision to the Fair Labor Standards Act requiring employers to provide breaks and a clean space for expressing milk, it only required that for large employers. And only a few states have lactation access laws.

**12.15** **D** is the best answer. The interviewer reacted negatively to the information Pete shared about his caregiving role and suggested that men aren't supposed to like children (or if they do, that it is an unsavory kind of liking) and the only time men would choose caregiving roles is if they were not capable of working.

**A** is not correct. This fact pattern reflects what is sometimes called "sex plus" discrimination. It is sex plus some other thing that the employer objects to. Here the "plus" is caregiving, which the interviewer perceives to be insufficiently manly. The comparator may share the same sex as Pete, but they don't share the "plus." Additionally, the simple fact of a caregiver in the same group would not automatically doom a case.

**B** is not correct because Title VII protects on the basis of sex. So, it protects members of all sexes, including men.

**C** is not correct because a difference in qualifications does not always point to discrimination.

**12.16** **B** is the best answer. Essentially, Quinta was seeking an accommodation—an exemption from the usual tardiness rules. The Pregnancy Discrimination Act only requires that employees be treated the same "as other persons not so affected but similar in their ability or inability to work." Quinta appears to have been treated the same as anyone else who was repeatedly tardy.

**A** is not correct. Work rules applied in a discriminatory manner can be challenged, and neutral work rules can be challenged under a disparate impact theory as well. Note that the fact pattern states that Quinta only brought a disparate treatment claim.

**C** is not correct. Even though morning sickness is a medical condition related to pregnancy, Quinta will only have a right to an accommodation if other employees are allowed to be tardy for other reasons.

**D** is not correct. Even though pregnancy was a but-for cause for the termination, it was a but-for cause for her tardiness, and that tardiness was a but-for cause for the termination. In other words, Quinta's employer was motivated by her tardiness, not by the reason that she was tardy—pregnancy.

**12.17** There is not necessarily a right answer to this question, which asks the reader to think deeply about the Court's reasoning in *Bostock* and its use of the but for test in its examples.

On the one hand, a person might conclude that bisexual people are not protected under Title VII because they engage in behavior that is both gender conforming and gender non-conforming. And they may be discriminated against not for that, but for not limiting their romantic attachments to a single sex. If that is the way we look at what bisexuality is, then both men who fail to limit their romantic attachments to one sex and women who fail to limit their romantic attachments to one sex will be treated the same way. Some men who date men will be fired, and so will some women who date men. If this is the analysis, it would seem that a bisexual (or pansexual) orientation would not be protected by Title VII.

On the other hand, people who are bisexual don't tend to be objected to until their same-sex affinity is revealed. In that framing, it's not bisexuality per se that an employer is discriminating against. Instead, it's the trait or chance of behavior that is not gender-conforming that triggers the discrimination. Thus, discrimination against bisexual people is exactly like discrimination against gay people and should be protected by the logic used in *Bostock*—but for the chance that this man might be romantically attracted to another man, he wouldn't have been fired.

Topic 13 Answers

# Focused Issues Related to Protected Classes: Religion

13.1 A is the best answer. Employers may not discriminate on the basis of religion, and Title VII defines religion as including all aspects of belief and practice. 42 U.S.C. § 2000e(j). An employer must accommodate an employee's religious practice, unless doing so poses an undue hardship. *Id.* Undue hardship is not a difficult standard. Anything more than de minimis will be an undue hardship. *Trans World Airlines, Inc. v. Hardison*, 432 U.S. 63 (1977). A states the rule correctly and is consistent with the facts. A potential loss of 3% of customers is more than de minimis.

B is not correct because the definition of religion is expansive. As the EEOC's website explains,

> For purposes of Title VII, religion includes not only traditional, organized religions such as Christianity, Judaism, Islam, Hinduism, and Buddhism, but also religious beliefs that are new, uncommon, not part of a formal church or sect, only subscribed to by a small number of people, or that seem illogical or unreasonable to others. An employee's belief or practice can be "religious" under Title VII even if the employee is affiliated with a religious group that does not espouse or recognize that individual's belief or practice, or if few—or no—other people adhere to it. Title VII's protections also extend to those who are discriminated against or need accommodation because they profess no religious beliefs.

*Questions and Answers: Religious Discrimination in the Workplace*, EEOC, https://www.eeoc.gov/laws/guidance/questions-and-answers-religious-discrimination-workplace. Thus, the fact that Alvin's religion may not be widely followed is irrelevant.

C is not correct because it misstates the BFOQ rule. The issue is not that customer preference would be a BFOQ, but a particular religion that would be a BFOQ.

D is not correct because it does not contain the complete rule. When a religious practice is at issue, it is not enough that the employee sincerely believes that they must engage in that practice.

**13.2** **D** is the best answer. This is another situation in which an employee is seeking an accommodation for a religious practice, and that accommodation would pose more than a de minimis hardship. That hardship can be economic, as in question 13.1, or it can be an increased burden on other employees. The fact that Mary and Joe also have religious rights adds a new aspect to this hypothetical, but it is not relevant for purposes of this question.

**A** is not correct for two reasons. First, members of a group can discriminate against fellow members. Secondly, a religious practice is specific to the person and not judged based on the tenets of the institution. Moreover, different sects of Christianity have different beliefs.

**B** is not correct because accommodations for one employee does not "discriminate" against other employees. It puts the accommodated employee on equal ground. At the same time, an accommodation for one employee that requires something from the employee's coworkers can create a hardship that will be undue.

**C** is not correct because it does not state a correct rule. Joe and Mary's grocery business may have some First Amendment rights, but the ministerial exemption only applies to churches and is not automatic, but only applies to decisions about ministers.

**13.3** **B** is the best answer. Section 702 (42 U.S.C. § 2000e-1) provides that Title VII

> shall not apply . . . to a religious corporation, association, educational institution, or society with respect to the employment of individuals of a particular religion to perform work connected with the carrying on by such corporation, association, educational institution, or society of its activities.

Temple Beth-el clearly qualifies for this exemption and can thus hire only co-religionists to run the daycare.

**A** is not correct because, while daycare workers could be ministers, that is a fact intensive question and not automatically true.

**C** is not the best answer because the fact that a religious educational institution might serve people of all religions doesn't affect its ability to claim the co-religionist preference under section 702.

**D** is not correct because the co-religionist preference does not require that the employees be engaging in religious work.

**13.4** Current law would not consider Craftsy, Inc. to be a religious corporation or organization, because it is a for-profit entity. *EEOC v. Townley Engineering & Manufacturing Co.*, 859 F.2d 610 (9th Cir. 1988). It might be tempting to think that the Supreme Court's decision in *Burwell v. Hobby Lobby Stores, Inc.*, 573 U.S. 682 (2014), would govern, and Craftsy would be considered a religious corporation entitled to the exemption. *Hobby Lobby* was a case interpreting the Religious Freedom Restoration Act, which describes those protected as "persons." Title VII doesn't use that terminology but is much more specific and narrow.

**13.5** **D** is the best answer. The ministerial exception is very, very broad in the sense that it provides an absolute exemption from lawsuits. It is narrow, though, in that it only applies to certain employers and only certain employees. It only applies to churches, religious orders, or organizations, like schools, run by churches or religious orders. And it only applies to those who fit the definition of "minister." The school here almost certainly qualifies, since it appears to be a school run by the Catholic church. The harder question is whether this soccer coach might be a minister. The test is fact intensive and depends on whether the institution holds out the person as a minister, whether the person needs some level of religious training, whether the employee considered themselves a minister, and whether the employee's duties reflect a role in conveying and carrying out the mission of the church. *Hosanna-Tabor Evangelical Lutheran Church & School v. EEOC*, 565 U.S. 171 (2012). It's not possible, based on this test, to completely rule out the possibility that the soccer coach could be a minister.

**A** is not correct because it does not foreclose finding that Alex might nonetheless be a minister. Additionally, it is possible that the school sees the skills connected with playing soccer and competing as bound up in its religious mission.

**B** is not correct because the ministerial exception is a defense to any kind of alleged violation of an employment law. It doesn't simply allow discrimination on the basis of religion.

**C** is not correct because Catholic schools may almost always, if not always, be eligible for claiming the ministerial exception, but that exception applies only to ministers. Not every employee will be a minister, necessarily.

**13.6** **C** is the best answer. This fact pattern reflects one of the most challenging current issues under Title VII. The religious organization exception allows religious institutions to discriminate on the basis of religion, which includes religious practices. So, a religious institution can require its employees to conform to a set of religious rules. Here, the school has said that his marriage violates its religious rules, which is discrimination on the basis of religion, even though the facts may also look like discrimination on the basis of sex.

**A** is not correct. The school is not treated like any other employer, but instead has some special exceptions under Title VII.

**B** is not correct. Even though it is a correct statement and application of the but-for test, the same conduct can be viewed as violating a religious rule, and there is an exception for religious institutions that allows them to discriminate on the basis of religion.

**D** is not correct because it overstates that exception. Churches are not allowed to discriminate on any basis other than religion. The challenge is where the religion has rules about sex, race, or national origin. Then that kind of discrimination seems to be able to be shoe-horned into the exception.

# Focused Issues Related to Protected Classes: Age

**14.1** C is the best answer. A covered employer violates the ADEA if it discriminates on the basis of age against people who are 40 or older. By targeting people in younger age groups for ads, it seems like Facebook might be preferring those under 40 and even within the protected group, those younger to those older. Because C is framed conditionally to satisfy this rule, it is the best answer.

A is not the best answer because it does not entirely negate the inference that targeting younger people is the goal.

B is not correct because it is not the rule for age-related disparate treatment, and because it assumes facts not in the fact pattern.

D is not the best answer because it does not provide the rule for disparate treatment, which this appears to be. Facebook is explicitly considering age, and can only do so if age is a BFOQ.

**14.2** A is the best answer because it correctly states the rule under the ADEA for disparate impact and its defense, "reasonable factor other than age." It is also consistent with the facts in the fact pattern. Musical taste does not seem relevant to a job unrelated to music of other eras. This job instead involves judgments about whether content violates Facebook's terms of service or community standards.

B is not correct because it does not provide the correct rule. BFOQ is a defense to disparate treatment, not disparate impact, and age must be the BFOQ.

C is not the best answer because disparate impacts based on age will also violate the ADEA.

D. I'm sorry. I couldn't resist.

**14.3** If this action was brought in Illinois, or any other state in the 7th Circuit, it would be dismissed. The Seventh Circuit has held that applicants cannot bring disparate impact claims under the ADEA. *Kleber v. CareFusion Corp.*, 914 F.3d 480 (7th Cir. 2019) (en banc).

**14.4** C is the best answer. This fact pattern gives us an omniscient view into the intent of the decision makers. We know that they want to make some employees leave because of their older age. That is clearly unlawful disparate treatment under the ADEA.

A is not the correct answer because the policy was adopted with the purpose that older workers be terminated. This intent is what matters, and the fact that the policy is not explicit about this intent does not negate that intent.

B is not the best answer because, even though employers are allowed to consider salary costs in making decisions, they considered age in this situation. That they had a further justification for why they picked age does not negate the fact that they intended to target older workers.

D is not correct because it appears to (somewhat incorrectly) provide a defense to disparate impact by focusing on something other than age that is, nonetheless, linked with age. That is not the cause of action that this fact pattern presents, and it is not the test for when a disparate impact will violate the ADEA.

**14.5** There are several ways that age differs from race, color, national origin, religion, and sex, and all of those are relevant. First, the classes protected by Title VII are viewed as immutable characteristics that, for the most part, are not relevant to a person's interest in or ability to perform any particular job. Moreover, these characteristics have historically been used to limit people's access to the political process. And while the terms are neutral and apply to everyone—everyone has a race or sex, for example—the groups within those classes are considered distinct and separate with firm boundaries. Blackness is a category separate from whiteness.

The status of being 40 years old or older—the group protected by the ADEA—is different. Everyone (who remains alive, of course) will move into this group, and so it seems strange to think about animus like race-based animus against the group existing. Additionally, as we age, our abilities change, and eventually, they decline. So, age may be relevant to ability. Moreover, because of the way that experience and seniority drive higher wages, older workers are more expensive. For these reasons, preferring relatively younger workers is often rational.

**14.6** This kind of policy question does not have a correct answer. Rather, the question seeks to probe a student's familiarity with the policies underlying the ADEA and other antidiscrimination laws as well as the specific findings of Congress in enacting the ADEA. Generally speaking, the best answers not only address policy issues that support their conclusion, but also acknowledge strong counterarguments and address them.

An answer that suggests this is an error that the Supreme Court should fix might focus on the practical effects of discrimination. Even if older workers in general have larger savings, for example, any particular older worker may not. Moreover, younger workers, presumably, have an easier time getting a new position and more time to build up their savings for retirement. Additionally, what might look at first glance like a positive stereotype might actually not be. In the sex stereotyping context, it does not seem that courts view so-called "positive" stereotypes as acceptable.

An answer that suggests this is not an error that the Supreme Court should fix might focus on either a lack of harm in positive stereotypes, or the benefits of waiting for Congress to act instead. The lack of harm in positive stereotypes might link discrimination only to those persistent negative views that create barriers for older workers in the labor market broadly. Perhaps those positive stereotypes do not have the same kind of market-wide effect. The concern about the Court acting instead of Congress might focus on the role of Congress in setting national policy, and providing clear guidance to employers.

# Focused Issues Related to Protected Classes: Disability

15.1 **False.** The ADA explicitly provides that "[a]n impairment that is episodic or in remission is a disability if it would substantially limit a major life activity when active." 42 U.S.C. § 12102(4). Thus, Jill is disabled within the meaning of the statute even though her seizures are under control.

15.2 **True.** The explicit provision on episodic impairments or impairments in remission was added to the ADA by the ADA Amendments Act of 2008. Without that language, the Supreme Court had held in *Sutton v. United Air Lines, Inc.*, 527 U.S. 471 (1999), that an impairment would not substantially limit a major life activity if the impairment is removed or significantly reduced through mitigating measures, like medication.

15.3 **True.** The ADA is much more nuanced in balancing interests of employees and employers, but also has explicit provisions banning employers from discovering information that might cause them to discriminate. Things like sex, race, color, and national origin, at least, are generally considered "chronically accessible" traits. That is, they are categories that quickly come to mind based on observation of a person's appearance and behavior. Some disabilities are readily apparent, but some are hidden or invisible. Thus, part of the ADA's purpose is to prevent the employer from discovering those invisible disabilities.

15.4 C is the best answer because it provides the correct rule for when an employer can terminate an employee with a disability. The duty an employer has toward a current employee is no different from the duty it has toward an applicant.

A is not correct because an employer need not retain an employee who cannot perform the essential functions of their position. Employers are required only to provide an accommodation that is reasonable and need not even do that if doing so would pose an undue hardship. Generally speaking, removing essential functions of a job and creating a new position are considered unreasonable.

B is not correct because the ADA does require the employer to provide a reasonable accommodation if it can do so without undue hardship.

D is not correct because the ADA is not structured as wage insurance the way that workers compensation is.

15.5 D is the best answer. The ADA explicitly provides that an employer

> may hold an employee . . . who is an alcoholic to the same qualification standards for employment or job performance and behavior that such entity holds other employees, even if any unsatisfactory performance or behavior is related to the . . . alcoholism of such employee.

42 U.S.C. § 12114(c)(4).

A is not correct because there is a special rule for the results of alcohol use, so the usual disability-related limits do not apply.

B is not correct because such notice is not required.

C is not correct because there is a special rule for the results of alcohol use even if the person has the disability of alcoholism.

**15.6** C is the best answer. Edward is actually disabled because when he is not medicated, he is substantially impaired in the major life activity of remaining conscious. More importantly for this fact pattern, Safeco regards Edward as having an impairment, and thus regards him as disabled. Refusing to hire him because it perceives him as having an impairment is disparate treatment under the ADA and unlawful.

An employer can refuse to hire someone whose disability would pose a direct threat to them or other employees. This is an affirmative defense. 42 U.S.C. § 12113(a), (b). "The term 'direct threat' means a significant risk to the health or safety of others that cannot be eliminated by reasonable accommodation." 42 U.S.C. § 12111(3). However, Edward's medication, according to the fact pattern (don't fight the hypothetical), is completely effective. Thus, his impairment is not a direct threat to either him or other workers.

A is not correct because Edward's medication is so effective that his impairment would not pose a direct threat to him or others.

B is not correct because, where an impairment is controlled by medication, we evaluate disability by looking at whether a person is disabled without that medication. Edward is clearly disabled. Moreover, this is not relevant if Edward's employer regarded him as having an impairment. The employer here clearly does.

D is not correct because Edward did not need an accommodation to do the job and was not seeking an accommodation.

15.7 B is the best answer because it provides for the two alternate ways the employer may be motivated to deny him his former position, states the correct rule, and is consistent with the facts. The station is at least considering Stan to be impaired because it considers him susceptible to a stroke. Susceptibility to a stroke, or a stroke itself, is an impairment to a person's vascular and neurological functioning, both major life activities. So, at the very least, the station regards Stan as disabled. It also may be concerned about people's memories of his past stroke. In that way, it may be motivated by his record of disability. Either way, it is motivated by that impairment or the record of his impairment, which is disparate treatment under the ADA.

A is not correct because Stan is not seeking an accommodation and does not need one. He can perform all of the essential functions of the anchor position, because he is fully recovered.

C is not correct for the same reason. Stan may be actually disabled if he continues to have an impairment to his vascular system, for example, but he can perform the essential functions of the job without an accommodation, and he is not seeking one.

D is not correct because Stan may be disabled if he continues to have an impairment to his vascular system. Moreover, even if he is no longer disabled, the station is regarding him as having an impairment based on his stroke or penalizing him for his record of having an impairment based on his stroke. Either leads to liability.

15.8 D is the best answer because it correctly states the law and is not inconsistent with the facts. If Bland wins, the only reason, of the four choices offered, would be that it can demonstrate that accommodating him would pose an undue hardship on the business. Undue hardship under the ADA is a more demanding standard than under Title VII's religion accommodation provision. So, the best argument that Bland could make is the financial burden of accommodating an exception to its shaving policy, and there is some evidence to demonstrate a potential financial burden.

A is not correct because the ADA explicitly provides that conditions that are episodic are still impairments even when the symptoms are not occurring.

B is not correct because the essential functions of the job are to sell clothing. Claude's impairment does not interfere with the tasks required for selling clothing, which most likely consist of moderate physical activities, communication skills, and ordinary cognitive skills.

C is not a correct application of the rules governing what counts as a major life activity. Major life activities include bodily organs and systems, and Claude's condition impairs the normal functioning of his skin and hair growth.

15.9 A is the best answer. The undue hardship standard under the ADA requires significantly more than de minimis hardship to provide a defense. The chance that one exception would cause 3% of customers to leave, even at one store, seems pretty small.

**B** is not the best answer because it does not reflect any rule connected with the ADA, and it is not clear that it would create any potential liability under the ADEA unless the policy is intended to exclude workers 40 and older.

**C** is not the best answer because it reflects the rule for sex-specific grooming codes, not grooming codes that affect persons with disabilities.

**D** is incorrect because the grooming code does not explicitly exclude people with disabilities, which is what "facially discriminatory" usually means. I apologize for the terrible pun.

**15.10** **B** is the best answer because it correctly states the rules regarding accommodations and is consistent with the facts. Of the potential reasons offered, it is the only one that correctly explains the rationale for how Amy could win.

The issue in this question is part of a current circuit split, about employers' obligations to reassign an employee to a vacant position as a reasonable accommodation. The ADA explicitly lists reassignment to a vacant position as a potential reasonable accommodation, 42 U.S.C. § 12111(9)(B), but does not give more guidance about how such a reassignment should work if there are other candidates for the position as well. The Seventh and Eighth Circuits don't require reassignment if the employer has a policy to pick the most qualified candidate and there is a candidate for that position more qualified than the employee who needs the reassignment as an accommodation. *EEOC v. Humiston-Keeling, Inc.*, 227 F.3d 1024 (7th Cir. 2000); *Huber v. Wal-Mart Stores, Inc.*, 486 F.3d 480 (8th Cir. 2007). The Tenth Circuit and D.C. Circuits require the employer to award the vacant position to the employee needing the accommodation as long as that employee is qualified. *Smith v. Midland Brake, Inc.*, 180 F.3d 1154 (10th Cir. 1999) (en banc), *Aka v. Washington Hospital Center*, 156 F.3d 1284 (D.C. Cir. 1998) (en banc). Complicating matters, the Seventh Circuit has walked back its approach, holding that employers can only choose the most qualified employee where reassignment of the employee with a disability would pose an undue hardship.

Both sides of the split read the Supreme Court's decision in *U.S. Airways v. Barnett*, 535 U.S. 391 (2002), differently. In *Barnett*, the Court said that the reasonable accommodation should ask whether the requested accommodation would, in the run of cases, be reasonable. And then the Court held that a reassignment which would violate an employer's seniority policy would not, in the run of cases, be reasonable because seniority has a special, privileged role in employment law and employer practices. The analysis in *Barnett* has been criticized as not following the very rule the Court laid out. It did not ask whether reassignment would be reasonable in the run of cases and then ask whether the presence of a seniority system would make reassignment of junior employees an undue hardship for this employer. Instead, the Court treated the accommodation as waiving operation of the seniority system. Ultimately courts now debate whether a "most qualified applicant" policy is more or less like a seniority system. And further complicating the issue, the ADA Amendments Act undercut other parts of the decision holding that such an accommodation is not reasonable.

A is not correct because it does not address the accommodations issue, and it's kind of a word salad. Amy is actually disable. If Superstore does not accommodate her when the accommodation would be reasonable and providing it would not be an undue hardship, Superstore will have engaged in disparate treatment.

C is not correct because paying a higher salary than a position warrants is almost certainly not a reasonable accommodation, both because of cost and because of disruption to coworkers and other aspects of the business that would follow in most workplaces. Amy is only entitled to the salary of the position she can perform.

D is not correct because the ADA does not impose different duties based on whether a person is a current employee or an applicant. That said, the status of a person may play into judgments of what is reasonable in the run of cases, and so it may have some effect. But regardless, Amy's qualifications are not irrelevant.

**15.11** The question of whether Superstore would have to provide a robot to help Amy would depend on a number of factors. Depending on factors like the location of Amy's work, the cost of the robot, and whether it might be useful for other employees, it could very well be reasonable to require such a robot in the run of cases. Superstore could argue that provision of such a robot would be an undue hardship to it even if providing one would ordinarily be reasonable, if Superstore was a smaller employer with a limited budget or there was something unique about the business that would make the robot disruptive.

**15.12** C is the best answer. The ADA prohibits employers from conducting medical examinations or making inquiries of applicants that could reveal that they are a person with a disability. Doing so is discrimination. 42 U.S.C. § 12112(d). Because the answers to some of the questions might reveal a person has a cognitive, emotional, or behavioral disorder, this test, given at this stage of the hiring process, would violate that provision.

A is not correct because it does not involve any rule or test connected with the ADA.

B is not correct because consent to discrimination is not a defense, and it is not clear that applicants really would satisfy the rules for consent.

D is not correct because it describes a defense to disparate impact. That defense is not available for pre-offer medical inquiries.

**15.13** A is the best answer because it correctly states the rule and is consistent with the facts. Kevin has an impairment that substantially limits the major life activity of maintaining balance. The Electric Company must provide a reasonable accommodation that allows him to perform the essential functions of his job unless doing so would pose an undue hardship. Removing an essential function of the job is not a reasonable accommodation, though, and that is what Kevin appears to be asking for.

B is not correct because the major life activity impacted isn't limited to working at heights.

C is not a correct analysis; an employer isn't required to remove an essential function of the job as an accommodation. That is, by definition, unreasonable. If a person is unable because of an impairment to perform the essential functions of a position, that person is not a qualified individual with a disability.

D is not correct because it does not correctly frame the direct threat defense. Additionally, the analysis need not get that far, because Kevin cannot perform the essential functions of the job.

**15.14** B is the best answer because it explains the rule for associational discrimination claims. The ADA prohibits discrimination against an employee because that employee is associated with someone who has a disability. And employers may not terminate employees because of that association even if they are also motivated by cost or concerns about productivity. The ADA was intended to limit employers' ability to make assumptions about those with disabilities and their family members.

A is not correct because the ADA doesn't provide this kind of general job security. It simply prohibits penalties when the decisionmaker is motivated by the child's disability.

C is not correct because the ADA does apply to adverse employment actions, even when they affect multiple employees.

D is not correct because the ADA provides a cause of action for associational disability discrimination in addition to discrimination against an employee for their own disability.

**15.15** C is the best answer. An employer is not required to remove an essential function of the job as an accommodation, and the work policy frames in-office work as an essential function. The employer gets some deference in defining the essential functions of the job, and it is a fact-intensive inquiry. The fact that the only exception to the policy was when courts were closed supports the employer's claim that in-person work is required.

A is not the best answer because Mark is still a person with a disability when he is in remission, and the transitory analysis for an impairment only applies if the impairment as a whole is likely to be minor and short lived. This is neither.

B is not a correct statement of the rule for when accommodations will pose an undue burden under the ADA. It may be for religious accommodations, however.

D is not correct because, even though the state itself may not be sued for damages under the ADA because of Eleventh Amendment limitations (assuming the state has not waived that immunity), individual officers may be sued for prospective injunctive relief through the *Ex Parte Young* exception. Moreover, even if states can't be sued by private parties, they still must comply with the ADA.

**15.16** D is the best answer. Even though it is possible that a court could find that working in the office is an essential function, it could also find that working in the office is not an essential function of this job. Facts that could support that finding are the predictability of the work, the fact that most of it can be done anywhere a person has access to a computer and the internet (or other sources for research), and the fact that it had been done in the past at least for short periods, which is all Mark is asking for.

A is not correct because the policy is not a per se violation of the ADA because it does not require anything that will always violate the ADA.

B is not a correct statement of any rule connected with the ADA.

C is not a correct statement of any rule, either, although the fact that employees were allowed to work from home temporarily is something a court could consider. That fact is not by itself determinative.

15.17 A is the best answer. An employer is required to engage in an interactive process with an employee who is disabled if it has concerns that she will not be able to perform the essential functions of the job or if she requests accommodations to allow her to do so. Simply assuming no accommodation is possible violates the ADA.

B is not correct because the employer is required to provide reasonable accommodations if it can do so without undue hardship.

C is not correct because it is unlikely that accommodation is impossible given Nell's high level of performance in the past. Additionally, even if that ends up being true, the employer needs to engage in the interactive process to reach that determination.

D is incorrect because Nell did not request any accommodations, and the cost (figuratively and literally) is unknown at this point.

15.18 This policy-type question requires students to think more deeply about how disability and the group protected by the ADA is different from the classes protected by Title VII and the ADEA. There is no particular right answer, but answers should explore the way that disparate impact and accommodation requests are functionally similar and the broad definition of disability.

In disparate impact cases, plaintiffs are often challenging employment practices or rules that have a disparate impact on them because of some disadvantage they face or experience, either because of discrimination or lack of equal access to something in some social context outside of this employer (like education) or because of physical differences (like those differences true in the aggregate between most women and most men). The point of that challenge is to change the practice or rule so that it does not disadvantage them. A request for accommodation is often a request to alter some employment practice or rule because of some disadvantage the plaintiff experiences because of an impairment. The point of that challenge is to change the practice or rule so that it does not disadvantage them. So, the functional goal is the same. And it is much easier to bring a case for a single individual to seek an exception for just them than it is to frame the remedy based on its impact on a larger class, defined by something that is not necessarily uniformly experienced by members of that group.

Relatedly, the disability community is a very large and diverse group with needs that are not uniform. In some ways, the fact that the disability rights movement has been a successful movement, at least at times, is a bit surprising because of the diversity of interests and needs of people who have disabilities. Without a cohesive, single experience, bringing an action on behalf of "people with disabilities" and showing how an employment practice uniformly affects those people (or disproportionately does so) is extremely challenging.

Answers might also point to the way that courts are skeptical of disparate impact liability as a reason these cases are not brough under the ADA, and other reasons as well.

# Sample Exam

## Answer 1.

## Alexa's claims

Alexa can bring a disparate treatment claim for race and sex discrimination in violation of Title VII, maybe even an intersectional claim, and she can do so by proving that, but-for her protected class, she would not have suffered an adverse employment action or that her race and sex were a motivating factor for the adverse employment actions she suffered. To the extent that her claim is focused on race, she might also be able to bring an action under 42 U.S.C. § 1981. An intersectional claim may be something of a challenge because § 1981 does not prohibit sex discrimination. But after the Court's expansive explanation of but-for causation in *Bostock v. Clayton County*, 140 S. Ct. 1731 (2020), some courts are recognizing intersectional claims when they involve the intersection of rights under two separate statutes (like Title VII and the ADEA), so this might also be a possibility. There is one additional complication. In a discrimination claim under Title VII, a plaintiff need only show their protected class was a motivating factor for the adverse employment action, but under § 1981, they must show that their protected class was a but-for cause of the adverse employment action.

Regardless of which law governs, the proof structure and analytical process is the same. There is no single proof structure that she would be limited to, but it is in her interests not to use the *McDonnell Douglas* proof structure or argue for mixed motives, but instead to look to the evidence as a whole to conclude that her protected class was a but-for cause of the adverse employment actions she suffered. The reasons for this will be woven into the analysis that follows.

Alexa might also bring a retaliation claim, but this claim is less strong because it is not clear she will be able to establish a prima facie case.

### *1. Disparate Treatment*

There is no question but that GitM is a covered employer because it has more than 500 employees, and there is no question that Alexa is an employee because the facts say she is.

In order to prove a disparate treatment claim, a plaintiff has to show that they 1. suffered an adverse employment action, 2. because of 3. a class protected by Title VII. This can be done in a number of ways. A court can look at the evidence as a whole to decide whether these elements have been proven, or it might use the *McDonnell Douglas* burden shifting method, although this is most often used at the summary judgment stage. For interests of completeness, both approaches will be considered.

Conventional wisdom suggests that the *McDonnell Douglas* framework was created to make it easier for plaintiffs to enforce their rights under Title VII. The plaintiff must prove a prima facie case, then the burden of production shifts to the defendant to produce evidence of a nondiscriminatory reason for its action, which the plaintiff can then prove is simply a pretext for discrimination. The prima facie case is flexible, and in a case like Alexa's might look something like this: 1. Alexa is a member of a protected class (sex, race); 2. she was qualified for her position and performing adequately (no indications of trouble with the quality of her work or violation of a work rule); 3. she suffered an adverse employment action (demand to withdraw the conference submission; termination); and 4. other papers were allowed to be published (withdrawal) and she was replaced or the employer kept looking for someone with a similar performance history and qualifications to do her work (termination).

Alexa will focus on her race and sex as the classes protected by Title VII. One thing to note in the analysis is that as a Black woman, Alexa is especially vulnerable to discrimination. The combination of marginalized identities means that while she might face "just racism" or "just sexism," she also faces a unique blend of racism and sexism together that particularly targets Black women (sometimes referred to as "misogynoir"). Courts sometimes struggle with intersectional claims, though, and may wish to separate out her claims into a sex claim and a race claim.

Alexa can also prove that she is well qualified and performing adequately. She is a research scientist. She co-created and co-led her research department, so her employer obviously felt she was qualified to be in leadership. She regularly publishes research with external co-authors, so she is well-respected in her field. Her research is also internally reviewed before publishing, and the review process generally goes smoothly and quickly. The only requested changes in the past have been to ensure no sensitive information about GitM is inadvertently shared, so there have been no past issues with the quality or subject matter of her research. There is no evidence of any past performance issues or professional discipline.

Alexa will argue that she suffered two adverse employment actions. First, Steve (head of AI) demanded she withdraw her research submission on racial bias in AI. And second, she was terminated.

Alexa probably can prove a prima facie case, but she might struggle a little on the fourth prong. The fact pattern says that the company announced research policy changes after Alexa was terminated. If those policy changes were in the works before the incident with Steve Smith, it might be challenging for Alexa to show that the demand to withdraw her paper wasn't part of a business-related redesign. Similarly, Alexa was sort of replaced, but the department was reorganized. And if Robert Cole is a replacement, he's a member of the same race, which could undercut Alexa's ability to link her race with the discharge decision.

There is one other challenge for Alexa related to her prima facie case. It's possible that the demand to withdraw her paper would not rise to the level of an adverse employment action. Title VII prohibits refusing to hire or to fire or otherwise discriminate in compensation or other "terms, conditions, or privileges" of employment. It's true that, in the past, the research scientists have published papers with outside researchers, but it's not clear from the facts that publishing is a part of Alexa's job or something GitM promised she could do in her job. Still, the fact that it was a common practice does suggest that publishing was something she expected to be able to do in connection with her work at GitM.

Assuming that Alexa can show a prima facie case for the demand that she withdraw her paper and her termination, GitM will have to provide a nondiscriminatory reason for its actions. Based on the fact pattern, it is likely that GitM will say that the reason that it asked Alexa to withdraw the paper was because it thought the study was poorly done and was "advocacy disguised as science." The claim about the quality of the paper is risky, because that claim might not be believed given Alexa's work in the past and the ability of others to read the paper and draw their own conclusions. GitM could even say that it just didn't like the study's conclusions and/or that the study undermined its product. Then when Alexa resisted, GitM fired her for not simply withdrawing the paper, or even because she tried to publish it. This may be a somewhat unflattering portrait of GitM in the court of public opinion, but it would be a nondiscriminatory reason that Alexa would have a hard time disproving.

Once GitM articulates a non-discriminatory reason, Alexa would provide evidence of pretext. And if she does not use the *McDonnell Douglas* framework, she will use all of this evidence to argue that, looking at the totality of the circumstances, GitM demanded she withdraw her paper and terminated her because of her race and sex.

Regarding the demand that she withdraw the paper, Alexa can point to the way that the demand conflicted with past practices on outside research. That casts doubt on most of the reasons that GitM will offer to justify its actions. Pulling Alexa's research based on quality concerns was inconsistent with past practices because Alexa's prior research projects always passed internal review and previous requested changes were only to protect sensitive information, so the employer obviously never had a problem with the quality or content of Alexa's previous research.

Comments connected with the Alexa's questions about the demand also show that race was on Smith's mind. First, Steve called her research "advocacy disguised as science." Alexa was drawing attention to the way facial recognition AI could have a negative disparate impact on dark-skinned people. Steve labelled that "advocacy," which suggests he viewed a mere description of race or color discrimination to be offensive. He was clearly offended or upset because, when Alexa asked if the same decision would have been made if Bell had written the paper, Smith reacted strongly, "exploding." Moreover, race was clearly the underlying offensive topic, since Alexa didn't bring up race in connection with Bell, but Smith responded by saying that she was creating a toxic environment always focused on race. His additional comments that followed implicated both race and sex, saying that the company had given her a chance no other company would have, presumably because of her race and sex because, "[h]ow many Black women have the budget and profile you do" because of her position at GitM which was the only reason she was getting conference invitations.

These comments would also be relevant to show that the reason for her termination was her race. She might argue that Smith reacted so strongly because she was a Black woman who was standing up for herself. And there were significantly more ways that race and sex would have been salient to put these comments and her treatment in context. Relevant to both adverse actions, Alexa had created the affinity group for Black engineers and researchers, which also may have been part of what Smith was thinking about when he talked about her creating a toxic workplace and focusing too much on race. Additionally, the demographic statistics of the employer bolster an inference that race and sex were the reason for Smith's actions. Only 4% of GitM's employees are Black and 6% are Latino. Only 1% of GitM's employees are Black women and 2% are Latina. Men outnumber women 2 to 1. Such a stark statistical demographic disparity shows that the company already has problems hiring and/or retaining minorities, specifically Black women. Finally, in the non-apology email, Smith acknowledged that firing Alexa had a particularly negative effect on women and Black employees. While that does not necessarily prove that race and sex were his motives for firing her, it does show that he understood what the demographics of the company meant for a sense of belonging for women and Black employees, at least at an intellectual level.

GitM would likely argue that the case shows mixed motives at best and that it would have taken the same actions without considering race and sex. First GitM would argue that the fact that Alexa was replaced by a Black man shows that it wasn't discriminating on the basis of race. And it might chalk up all of Smith's behavior and the adverse employment actions to concerns about Alexa undercutting a key product. It will be challenging to explain away Smith's comments, but they were not wholly focused on race, and so a jury might agree that those were just unfortunate comments that Smith didn't really mean.

### *2. Retaliation*

Alexa could try to bring a retaliation claim. Under Title VII (retaliation is also prohibited under § 1981), an employer may not retaliate against an employee opposing an unlawful employment practice. For retaliation, a plaintiff must show but-for causation and cannot use the mixed motives model. Alexa will have to show that (1) she suffered a materially adverse employment action (termination) (2) because of (3) protected activity (opposition conduct).

Alexa's retaliation claim would most likely point to her termination rather than the demand she withdraw her paper. The paper focused on discrimination in facial recognition in general, not discrimination at GitM. So the paper is not likely to be protected opposition conduct. Her question, though, about whether the same thing would have happened if Bell had submitted the paper might be protected opposition conduct. Alexa likely brought up Bell to say that GitM was only demanding the paper be withdrawn because Alexa was Black. That's certainly how Smith interpreted her question. If the withdrawal demand was made because Alexa was Black, that action would probably have violated Title VII, and so as long as Alexa's belief about the racial motivation behind the demand was reasonable, her question was protected opposition conduct. And because the conversation escalated from there and focused on race, it seems that Smith believed that she had objected to something that would violate Title VII. The termination seems to have been entirely precipitated by her question, and so the causal nexus seems clear, and Alexa would have a fairly strong retaliation claim—assuming that a reasonable person would believe that the demand to withdraw the paper was an adverse employment action.

## Bell's Claims

While Alexa will likely prevail on her disparate treatment claim and perhaps a retaliation claim, Bell will probably not be successful on her claim. Bell can bring a retaliation claim, but she will likely not prevail because the manner in which she opposed discrimination made her conduct unprotected.

Bell, too engaged in opposition conduct: by tweeting and by collecting information about discrimination against Alexa. If Bell only tweeted, she might have a very good retaliation claim. She acted in response to Alexa's termination and seems to have believed that it was discriminatory. Her tweet focused on the company's actions toward Black women and criticized its diversity efforts. A reasonable person would likely think that what happened to Alexa violated Title VII, the tweet clearly opposes what happened (and other discrimination), and so is likely protected conduct.

It isn't entirely clear that Bell was terminated because of the tweet, though. GitM publicly said the termination was because Bell had violated the code of conduct, which could be a veiled reference to the tweeting and public statements, but it also said that the termination had been for violation of the security policies by "exfiltration of confidential business-sensitive documents and private data of other employees." This appears to refer to gathering emails, which presumably were from or between employees other than Bell and which likely contained sensitive information. When the manner of opposition interferes with "management prerogatives," that opposition will not be protected. In other words, the opposition clause doesn't protect an employee who engages in insubordination, or disruptive or nonproductive behavior at work. *See McKennon v. Nashville Banner*, 513 U.S. 352 (1995). The collection of this information may thus be unprotected, and as a result, a nonretaliatory reason for Bell's discharge. And since mixed motives liability is not available in retaliation claims, this may effectively insulate GitM from liability, even if part of the reason that it terminated Bell was because of her public statements.

## Answer 2.

*This question on how to handle conflicts between protected classes or within Title VII calls on the writer to weigh in on policies on how to interpret the statute and has no correct answer. Many reasonable approaches could be taken, and this answer is just one example.*

Title VII conflicts—particularly between different religions or between religion and another protected class—should be handled on a case-by-case basis, with careful consideration of the interests at stake and harms that could result. Additionally, courts should, when making these decisions, also consider the purposes of Title VII and whether a decision would promote or hurt these purposes.

The first example given is that of a person whose religious practice requires them to evangelize, which may interfere with others' beliefs: following other religions, following no religion, or even a person with the same religion who does not feel compelled to evangelize. I think that current law on religious accommodation, harassment, and coercion in the workplace effectively strikes the right balance, mostly by deferring to the balance that employers strike and preventing coercion by supervisors or management.

Consider the choice of preventing a person from evangelizing at work or allowing employees to be evangelized to while working. Under the Supreme Court's decision in *TWA v. Hardison*, 432 U.S. 63 (1977), a requested religious accommodation (allowing evangelizing) would be an "undue hardship" if it causes "more than a de minimis cost." And an employer need not accommodate an employee in situations where other employees will be annoyed or disadvantaged by the accommodation. In situations like this, where allowing one practice could cause difficulty for other employees, the current state of the law puts the rest of the office's rights first. At the same time, if the level of evangelizing was very low or would not bother other employees, an employer could accommodate it without much risk that doing so would lead to liability. The standard for harassment is that the evangelizing would have to be so severe or pervasive that a reasonable person would find the environment abusive. This may be easier to satisfy where the evangelizing touches on matters of sex roles and gender, though. Lastly, where supervisors, management, or owners are the ones who wish to impose religious beliefs on employees below them, courts are more sympathetic to the employees because of the power held by supervisors, management, and owners. *See EEOC v. Townley Eng'g & Mfg. Co.*, 859 F.2d 610 (9th Cir. 1988).

The second example given is that an employer's right to practice religion might interfere with rights against sex or race discrimination. Title VII only allows certain religious entities to discriminate on the basis of *religion*, but because the definition of religion is so broad, it may open the door to allow employers to impose their views of how members of protected classes ought to behave. In these situations, the exemption should be interpreted narrowly. Title VII protects employees from employers and not the other way around. Any protection of the religious rights of employers should be interpreted as narrowly as the First Amendment will allow. Harm to third parties—here employees—should be minimized.

In addition to weighing harm done to individuals or groups, courts should also look at the intent of Title VII and the harm certain rulings might do to Title VII and to society as a whole. Title VII was enacted to promote equal treatment and equal opportunity; to remedy continuing effects of inequality and avoid perpetuating systems of oppression. Courts should sincerely consider the impact of allowing an employer with religious beliefs that counsel sex or race discrimination on the system as a whole. While I hesitate to use a slippery-slope argument, it is important to recognize that, in some situations, the public interest and overall importance in keeping Title VII effective in a pluralistic society, protecting groups who have historically and still do face inequality outweighs a religious belief that interferes with those protections.

## Answer 3.

Title VII explicitly prohibits refusing to hire someone because of their race or color. Given this language, the casting call seems really problematic. Whiteness is a race, defined in part by skin color, so an employer shouldn't be able to discriminate against white people simply because they are white. Additionally, covered entities cannot publish ads expressing that kind of discriminatory preference, so the ad itself seems to violate Title VII.

Title VII does contain some exceptions, though. Through the BFOQ, it allows some disparate treatment. And in that case, it's also fine to tailor an advertisement to fit.

But race and color can't be BFOQs. The statute explicitly only allows that defense for sex, religion, or national origin discrimination. And although national origin can be a BFOQ, that BFOQ is interpreted extremely narrowly because national origin includes ethnic heritage and overlaps with our concept of race.

At the same time, it seems like there ought to be an exception for casting. Imagine casting only white actors in *Roots*, a miniseries about enslaved persons and their descendants. The law that has developed around the BFOQ exception has significant appeal in the casting context. One situation where sex, religion, and national origin are sometimes considered bona fide occupational qualifications is when membership in that class is "necessary for the purpose of authenticity or genuineness, . . . e.g., an actor or actress." While race may be irrelevant to some casting decisions, as the *Roots* example shows, race matters when a show tells the story of real people who are known to be members of one race or when the production integrates race into the story itself. In those situations, race-based casting seems not only justified, but essential.

Even if a BFOQ was available and the authenticity exception applied, though, *Hamilton* still isn't a great fit. Most of the people portrayed in the musical were white in real life. So, a traditional claim to authenticity would seem to call for white actors. But the creators of the musical have turned the authenticity question on its head. The music comes from a primarily African-American cultural tradition. So, if the *way* of telling the story is what matters for authenticity, the call for performers of color has more appeal.

There is a third way that authenticity might matter: race itself is central to the message. Lin-Manuel Miranda, the creator of *Hamilton*, intended to use race to say something important about the founding generation and about this country now. Representation matters: if you can see yourself in the Founders, their struggles are more relatable and today's social challenges get a new context. Also, if you can see yourself in the role of people so central to what it means to be an American, you can see yourself as having a role to play as a citizen now, helping to create a better future.

Outside of the BFOQ and authenticity exception, the lack of diversity in the performing industry seems important. While the casting call might seem like a version of the "help wanted, white only" ads from the Jim Crow era, which Title VII was clearly designed to prohibit, the U.S. has no similar history where white people have been systematically and structurally excluded from employment opportunities. The opposite is true. The performing industry is very white-dominated, as the #OscarsSoWhite campaign shows.

Given the lack of diversity in the entertainment industry, maybe affirmative action would have been a better framing. Musicals like *Hamilton* give performers of color work they wouldn't otherwise have. Race-based affirmative action doesn't violate Title VII if the purpose of the measure is to provide opportunities in jobs where there is a manifest racial imbalance between those in the jobs and the those in the labor pool and where the measure doesn't unnecessarily trammel on the interests of white employees. *Hamilton* seems to fit this definition. The lack of opportunity for performers of color is well-documented. And one musical hardly makes a dent in the overall opportunities for white performers. Also, the casting call doesn't bar white performers, it just encourages non-white performers to audition. It's a more robust affirmative action statement than usual. Plus, there are lots of behind-the-scenes jobs connected with Hamilton. Presumably, overall, there are many opportunities for white applicants to work on the musical.

As a strategic matter, it's understandable why the company didn't mention affirmative action as the justification for the casting call. It carries so much political and social baggage. BFOQ may not be a good legal fit, but it sounds very legitimate and doesn't have the negative baggage.

# Additional Issue Spotter Questions

## Answer 1.

Okoro may have disparate treatment claims on the basis of religion (as a failure to accommodate claim) and national origin. She may have a retaliation claim, and she may have a harassment claim on the basis of religion and national origin.

*Disparate Treatment—Religious Discrimination*

Okoro may have a cause of action for disparate treatment based on religious discrimination. Title VII protects employees from discrimination on the basis of religion and defines religion to include religious practices in addition to beliefs. In order to state a cause of action, she must show that: (1) she has a sincerely held religious belief that conflicts with a job rule or requirement; (2) she told her employer, Younkers, about the belief (or it had reason to know); and (3) she was disciplined for failing to comply with the rule or requirement.

Here, Okoro's belief that she needs to wear a head covering is likely sincerely held. There are no facts to suggest that she *isn't* sincere, and a jury would also find her believable because wearing a hijaab or khimar is a practice associated with Islam. Okoro is a practicing Muslim. A religious practice isn't required to be widely shared to be protected, but the fact that it is often supports a credibility assessment.

Younkers might try to undermine her assertion that her belief is sincere that wearing a hijab is required because it is a new belief for Okoro. Up to this point, Okoro had not felt compelled by her faith to wear the hijab. However, this argument likely to fail because Okoro now sincerely believes that she must wear a hijab as part of her expression of faith. There is no requirement that people's religious beliefs must be uniform throughout their lives. The only question is whether Okoro is sincere that her religious practice is mandatory.

Next, Okoro must show that she told Younkers about the belief or practice. This will be simple for her to prove because she told Smith, her supervisor, that she would begin wearing a hijab. Next, Okoro must show that she was disciplined for failing to comply with the store's grooming code. Causation is pretty straightforward here. Okoro was told she could not wear the hijab under the store's grooming code, and she was fired two days after she began wearing it for a violation of the grooming code. Okoro will most likely be able to establish a prima facie case here.

Younkers has an affirmative defense to a religious accommodations claim. It will have to show that it either offered Okoro a reasonable accommodation or that it could not accommodate her because doing so would pose an undue hardship. An undue hardship in the religion context is anything more than a de minimis burden. The only reasonable accommodation in this case would be to allow Okoro to wear a headscarf, because it is a required expression of her Muslim faith.

Younkers did not even attempt to do this; therefore, their only defense is undue hardship. Here, Younkers will likely not be able to prove undue hardship even though the de minimis burden standard is so low. Smith's reasoning for not allowing Okoro to wear the hijab was that she was just following company policy and that having an employee with a hijab may hurt sales. Although the standard for undue hardship is low, a potential for lost sales with no evidentiary support is likely to fail. Reading the grooming code as a whole, it seems that the policy's purpose is to have employees appear professional. There is nothing inconsistent with a hijab and a professional appearance. Moreover, the head covering ban was on a list of things that included clothing that was more revealing or more casual than the image Younkers wanted to convey. A hijab does not fit within those categories. It is less revealing, and not casual the way a baseball cap or hat might be. It is possible that there might be some leeway surrounding what color or maybe material the headscarf is, but the scarf will have to comply with Okoro's beliefs. Moreover, it seems like Smith was making assumptions about customer preference in her assessment of whether an exception to the policy should be made. Even though BFOQ isn't quite the same analysis as a failure to accommodate claim, it seems like customer prejudice should not be able to create the kind of more-than-de-minimis hardship that will excuse an employer from having to accommodate an employee's religious practices.

Okoro will likely win a claim for disparate treatment based on religious discrimination.

### *Disparate Treatment—National Origin*

Okoro may have a claim for disparate treatment based on national origin. National origin refers to ethnic heritage or ancestry and does not require connection to any nation state. National origin discrimination frequently includes language and accent discrimination. The "convincing mosaic" method of proof is best for analyzing this cause of action, because there was a myriad of circumstantial evidence to show discrimination on the part of Okoro's supervisor, Smith.

Okoro must show that an adverse employment action was taken and that Younkers was motivated at least in part by her protected class. Here, Okoro would present evidence of Smith reprimanding her for speaking Igbo on the sales floor, snapping at her to "speak English!" even though she only spoke English to Smith, and the fact that Okoro speaks with an accent even though she speaks fluent English. The adverse employment action was that she was fired. Although the facts imply that she was fired for insubordination, or for breaking the work rule by wearing a hijab, a disparate treatment plaintiff must only show that their protected class was a motivating factor in the adverse employment action. Okoro could argue that her national origin, and one instance of speaking Igbo, made Smith get more punitive towards Okoro, culminating in the discharge eventually.

Younkers could argue that none of the conduct short of the termination would amount to an adverse employment action, and that Okoro cannot disprove that the reason for the termination was her violation of the grooming code. In fact, even if Okoro could show that national origin was a motivating factor, Younkers could show that it would have terminated her for violating the work rule, regardless of her national origin. Maybe Younkers could also argue that speaking English on the sales floor is a BFOQ for the position (because language is so tied to national origin, sometimes discriminating on the basis of language is national origin discrimination, and so language is what would be the BFOQ defense). The challenge here is that Okoro did speak English all of the time to English-speaking customers and employees.

Okoro would most likely not win a disparate treatment claim based on national origin. It is unclear whether the adverse employment action, her firing, was taken because of her speaking Igbo on the sales floor. If it was, Younkers would most likely be able to avoid damages by claiming a mixed motives defense.

### *Harassment—Race, Religion, and National Origin*

Okoro could also have a claim for harassment based on race and national origin and religion. To prove her prima facie case, she must show that she: (1) was exposed to conduct; (2) that conduct was unwelcome; (3) that she suffered a tangible employment action or that the conduct was severe or pervasive enough to create an abusive environment (an objective and subjective determination); and (4) something to suggest that her protected class was the reason for the conduct.

The conduct Okoro was exposed to was Smith yelling "speak English!," telling her she looked like a "terrorist sympathizer," and telling her to "leave the jungle at home."

Okoro would then have to show that this conduct was unwelcome. This is a mostly subjective determination, and Okoro would be able to prove this because of the racist content and the focus on her language or accent. A reasonable factfinder could easily believe that this kind of hostile, and humiliating conduct was unwelcome.

Okoro would have to argue that she either suffered a tangible employment action or that the conduct was severe OR pervasive enough to create an abusive environment. The harassment did culminate in her termination, and in some ways caused it by prompting a particular response in her. Those facts, that the conduct by Smith was all part of an ongoing campaign of harassment and hostility toward Okoro, could link the termination to that pattern of conduct sufficiently. However, because her termination was more linked to insubordination and wearing a headscarf, it might be easier for her to argue that the conduct was severe or pervasive enough that a reasonable employee would perceive it to be an abusive working environment.

First, Smith said "speak English" every day for three weeks, even though Okoro was already speaking English. It is not entirely clear that every day for three weeks would be long enough on its own to make the harassment pervasive, but it was also severe. Harassment will be severe when it is physically threatening or humiliating, intimidating or extremely hostile.

Smith's conduct was definitely intimidating, hostile, and humiliating, even if not necessarily physically threatening. Yelling at someone to "speak English" when they are, is highly humiliating, implying that they cannot be understood, or do not belong in an English-speaking space. In addition, Smith invoked particularly hostile imagery, linking Okoro's desire to wear a hijab to terrorism and telling her to "leave the jungle" at home.

Okoro would, at the very least, be able to prove a pervasive, abusive environment because a reasonable person in her position, considering all the circumstances, would likely find this environment to be hostile, and Okoro did in fact find it to be hostile.

Okoro would then have to show that the reason for the conduct was her race, religion, and national origin. This will be simple to prove because Smith only told her to "speak English" because of her accent, and called her a terrorist sympathizer, linking the hijab and Islam to terrorism. Moreover, the statements about the jungle and about "oogity boogity nonsense" all invoke negative stereotypes about Africans and Black people. These are humiliating references linked with race, religion, and national origin.

Younkers might argue that it should not be liable for this harassment because Okoro did not report it. Evaluating this defense is a bit of a challenge, because the fact pattern does not give us any information on Younkers' harassment policy or even if it had one. Okoro might be excused for not reporting if her termination is viewed as the culmination of the harassment. And even if it is not, she may be excused, depending on what that policy provides, whether reporting would have been futile, and possibly for not having time to report before she was terminated.

One additional note. Because race and national origin are implicated in Okoro's harassment and potential disparate treatment claim, she may have an action under 42 U.S.C. § 1981 in addition to a Title VII claim. That action would not require exhaustion of administrative remedies, and there are no damages limitations on her remedy. At the same time, Okoro would only have to prove that her national origin was a motivating factor in the harassment and adverse employment action for the disparate treatment claim under Title VII, but for § 1981, would have to prove national origin was a but-for cause.

### *Retaliation*

Okoro may have a retaliation claim against Younkers. To prove a prima facie case, Okoro must show that she: (1) engaged in protected activity; (2) that Younkers took a materially adverse employment action against her; and (3) that there is a causal link between the two events.

Okoro would first show that she filed a charge of religious discrimination with the EEOC and MCHR. This constitutes participation conduct, and Younkers is prohibited from discriminating against her because she has filed a charge. Okoro could also say that wearing her headscarf was protected opposition conduct because it was a response to discriminatory conduct. Opposition conduct will be protected as long as the employee has a reasonable good faith belief that what they oppose would have violated Title VII. The employee does not have to be correct as an absolute matter, but the failure to accommodate and harassment analyses above demonstrate that her belief that she had been discriminated against was reasonable. And the manner in which the employee opposes discrimination is not strictly limited. Opposition conduct will be protected unless the employee does something illegal or deliberately disrupts the work environment. Wearing a hijab is neither of these things.

Next, Okoro would show that Younkers took a materially adverse action against her because of her participation or opposition conduct. Here, Younkers fired her. That is clearly a materially adverse action.

Younkers might argue that Okoro cannot prove causation because the firing was linked to Okoro's violation of a work rule, which it might argue is not protected opposition conduct. And the only evidence that the termination was caused by Okoro's participation conduct was the timing—that it occurred after that conduct—but not so immediately after than an inference of causation could be drawn.

Here, Okoro would argue that her participation conduct was the real reason for the termination, pointing to the fact that Smith began her campaign of hostility right after she was interviewed by the HR director. That whole campaign of hostility culminated in Okoro's termination, and each step is linked in a continuous chain of events. Even if a court would not find that it was the participation conduct that caused the termination, Okoro's argument about wearing the hijab as protected opposition conduct is a good one, as well. Even though doing so may have broken a work rule, wearing a hijab is simply not analogous to the kinds of disruptions or insubordinate actions that will remove opposition conduct from the protection of the statute. She didn't take confidential documents, share confidential information, damage employer property, or anything similar.

Alternatively, Okoro might argue that the hostile environment that Smith created immediately after Okoro's participation conduct was itself an adverse employment action. Even if that harassment would not itself be actionable, it might be enough to constitute unlawful retaliation. The test for a sufficient adverse action under the retaliation provision is whether the employer's action is material, and it is material if it would deter a reasonable employee from taking the action they did. Three weeks of increasingly hostile behavior with no respite in sight may very well be enough to deter a reasonable employee from filing a charge.

Okoro is likely to win her retaliation claim against Younkers.

### *Disparate Impact—Religion*

In order to prevail on a disparate impact claim based on religion, Okoro must prove a prima facie case of discrimination by pinpointing the specific employment practice that results in a disparate impact, and then compare statistics regarding who "wins" under that practice and who is eligible for "winning."

Okoro would first state that the specific practice that causes a disparate impact is Younkers' dress code, which does not allow head coverings. Then, Okoro would have to show that this specific practice causes a disparate impact on Muslim women. This practice of not allowing head coverings would exclude 43% of Muslim women in the region and 0% of Christian women, who do not wear head coverings as part of their religious practice. In other words, 100% of Christian women would win, whereas only 57% of Muslim women would win. The EEOC's

4/5 rule states that when a selection rate for any group is less than 80% of the group with the highest rate, it will generally be considered evidence of adverse impact. It would not be erroneous to consider broader population data here instead of the actual applicants who applied, because hypothetically, an applicant could see the dress code and discern whether or not they would apply to a job that would not allow them to practice their faith. Additionally, this isn't a position that is highly skilled, so that suggests general population figures are appropriate for the labor pool.

Younkers would then bear the burden of proof for the affirmative defense of business necessity. It might choose to defend its grooming code as a whole as job related for the position of salesperson and a business necessity for that position. That is not a bad argument. Certainly a neat and professional appearance, part of a store's brand, plays a role in its success at sales. If this were the practice that Younkers focused on, Okoro could still prevail by showing the availability of an alternative practice which serves the employers needs but does not have the discriminator effect. The alternative practice Okoro would identify would be to have Younkers allow hijabs under the policy. This would serve Younkers' needs sufficiently in having a neat and professional appearing sales team, since hijabs conform to those requirements. Accordingly, Okoro would prevail. If the employment practice Younkers chose to defend was its decision to ban hijabs, the store would have a much harder time demonstrating business necessity. The only suggestion made about hijabs was the pure speculation by Smith that having salespeople with hijabs might lose the store profits. That is too speculative to satisfy the employer's burden. Without evidence, Younkers would lose the affirmative defense.

Okoro will likely win her disparate impact based on religion claim. It does not appear that Younkers would have any defense for its practice of disallowing religious head coverings.

## Answer 2.

Rhonda appears to have a cause of action for discrimination on the basis of sex and race for her discipline and effective termination (assuming she does not change her hair style). There is no real question about why she was disciplined. Her manager sent her home because he believed that her appearance violated the store's sex-specific grooming code. If that grooming code was discriminatory or interpreted in a discriminatory manner, then her discipline will violate Title VII.

Even though most explicit sex based rules will be direct evidence of disparate treatment, those rules in grooming codes are treated differently. A grooming code may make different rules for different sexes, but that grooming code will violate Title VII if it imposes an undue burden on one sex. This scenario is different from *Jespersen v. Harrah's Operating Co.*, 444 F.3d 1104 (9th Cir. 2006) (en banc), the most frequently cited case on sex specific grooming codes, in that in addition to having sex specific rules, it has a negative impact on some Black women, whose natural hair will not comply with the policy. It is not clear how this would be analyzed, exactly, so I'll analyze the issue using a grooming codes analysis, a disparate treatment framework, and a disparate impact framework.

Rhonda will argue that the grooming code poses an undue burden on women, but it is not clear that will be successful. Looking at the policy as a whole, there is not much that is different between men and women: maybe longer sleeves, women can wear skirts but men cannot, women can wear a bit more jewelry, women's hair may be dyed but men's may not, and hair length is different. Requiring that women have longer hair, falling below the collar, is the only requirement that would seem to require more, at least for some women, but not necessarily significantly more in terms of money or time.

The requirement that hair fall below the collar does impose an undue burden on Rhonda, though, because of her race. The cost of straightening or hair pieces, and the physical toll those take on her could be documented to demonstrate that burden. Additionally, it stereotypes the look that a woman should have. The policy provides that women's hair must be longer than the collar, however men working for employer can have hair that is no longer than their collar. This policy distinguishes between the two sexes under traditional stereotypical notions that men should have short hair and women should have long hair. This is a prescriptive stereotype that punishes Rhonda for not fitting into the mold of a what a woman traditionally should look like, similar to *Price Waterhouse v. Hopkins*, 490 U.S. 228 (1989). In fact, Rhonda's manager called her hairstyle unfeminine, suggesting he was acting because she didn't conform to sex stereotypes. At the same time, the policy doesn't overly sexualize women, which has been held to create an undue burden; in fact, the goal of the policy is modesty. It may still be problematic, though, analogous to cases where women were not trusted to make clothing decisions that men were trusted to make.

Still, it seems that the grooming policy is discriminatory against Rhonda on the basis of sex *and race*. It's because of a race-linked trait that she can't conform to a particular sex stereotype. So, a disparate treatment framework may be the appropriate one rather than the undue burden standard used for sex-specific grooming standards. As the courts held in *Rogers v. American Airlines*, 527 F. Supp. 229, 232 (S.D.N.Y. 1981), and *EEOC v. Catastrophe Management*, 852 F.3d 1018 (11th Cir. 2016), an employer who prohibits protective hairstyles often worn by Black people, like locs, twists, or braids, does not necessarily engage in disparate treatment on the basis of race. But those courts noted the case would be different if employers prohibited Afro hairstyles, or other immutable race-linked characteristics.

Rhonda's natural hairstyle, without the chemicals or hair pieces, seems like it would be so connected to her race that it would be race based disparate treatment to fire her for it. Even more clearly race-focused was the manager's interpretation of Rhonda's highlights as "extreme" and thus a violation of the policy. Blonde hair is a natural color of hair, and plenty of white women dye their hair blonde or have blonde highlights. If hair can be dyed, dying it a natural color does not seem to be extreme. To interpret blonde as extreme for a Black woman treats that woman differently from white women. Additionally, Rhonda's natural hair color is very light brown, making blonde highlights even more natural-appearing and less extreme.

To the extent that race-based disparate treatment is alleged, Rhonda can bring a claim under Title VII and 42 U.S.C. § 1981, and the legal analysis is roughly the same. To the extent that this is an intersectional claim, that might be challenging for a § 1981 claim, which prohibits race discrimination, but not sex discrimination. Still, this might be framed as a "race plus" case under § 1981 in the sense that the hair length requirement is disparate treatment against a subset of Black employees, Black women. But-for her race, Rhonda would not have been subject to discipline. Under § 1981, Rhonda would have to prove that race was a but-for cause, but under Title VII, only that it was a motivating factor in the discipline.

In addition, because the grooming policy doesn't explicitly mention race but fewer Black women can follow it than white women, the policy might be challenged as causing a disparate impact. That can only be brought under Title VII. Section 1981 only prohibits disparate treatment, not disparate impact. We don't have figures to do the disparate impact analysis, but it seems likely that the policy would disparately affect people with African heritage and any other ethnic groups that tend to have extremely curly hair. OTD would have to show that its grooming code policy, including the hair length requirement for women, was job related and a business necessity. It seems unlikely that it would be able to do so. There is nothing about selling home goods that requires women to have hair that extends beyond their collar. It's possible OTD might try to defend the grooming policy as a whole as job related and consistent with business necessity—that the customers expect workers to be dressed in a general modest fashion and groomed in a conservative, traditional, gender-conforming manner. If that were to be accepted as a business necessity, Rhonda could prove that allowing Black women to have short Afro-style hair, dyed only in colors that are natural hair colors for people, could be allowed under the policy.

OTD may want to argue that its dress code is justified by its exercise of religion. That was asserted by the manager who disciplined Rhonda. Title VII has exemptions for certain "religious corporations" and religious organizations. Some can discriminate on the basis of religion in hiring, and for some religiously controlled entities, certain employment matters are completely insulated from the protections of employment discrimination law.

The most protective doctrine is the ministerial exception, which provides that courts may not interfere with a church's decisions about its ministers. Even though this doctrine has been extended beyond churches to schools with religious missions, it seems unlikely that a for-profit entity could claim to be that kind of religious entity. If it could, it might argue that its salespeople are ministers, since they fulfill the store's religious mission. I am extremely skeptical that this would be successful, though. That would seem to go beyond what the Supreme Court has allowed to date. Although the Court has recognized that for-profit entities can be persons who exercise religious rights for purposes of some laws, treating them as churches is entirely different.

Title VII has exceptions within it for religious organizations or other religiously-motivated decisions. For example, religious organizations can discriminate on the basis of religion in hiring. And religion includes not just belief but religious practices. So an organization that qualifies under Title VII might be able to require employees to conform to particular religious rules for appearance and behavior.

It is unlikely that OTD would be considered a religious organization under Title VII. The courts to consider the issue so far, and the EEOC itself, exclude for-profits from the definition. Moreover, even if OTD could be considered a religious organization, if its grooming code were not enforced evenly to Black and white workers (and workers of all races), that different enforcement would constitute race discrimination, which religious employers are not allowed to engage in.

The last defense within Title VII is the BFOQ exception. If religion is a bona fide occupational qualification for a particular position, then an employer can discriminate in favor of that religion. Here, OTD might have something of an argument, but again, it seems a stretch. Because the store has a religious mission, it might argue that conforming to certain religious rules of behavior is essential for that mission. Still, it seems unusual to say that selling home goods would require particular religious behavior.

I guess there is one additional option. In *Bostock v. Clayton County*, 140 S. Ct. 1731 (2020), the Supreme Court left open the possibility that the Religious Freedom Restoration Act might provide a defense to any religiously-motivated discrimination. If the EEOC were to bring this action, that might apply. But it likely would not affect an action brought by Rhonda herself.

## Answer 3.

Higgins might have two disparate treatment claims: a pay claim and a promotion claim, both on the basis of race. Note that because these are race discrimination claims, they can be brought under both Title VII and 42 U.S.C. § 1981. The analytical structure is the same for both statutes, so even though Title VII is the statute discussed, the same analysis would apply for § 1981, as well, although the causation standard is a little different. For a Title VII claim, the plaintiff only has to prove that their race was a motivating factor, while under § 1981, they must prove that it was a but-for cause.

### *Pay Discrimination*

When the new brewery manager reclassified the line supervisors, he effectively reduced their pay. A pay cut is an adverse employment action under Title VII, actionable if taken for a prohibited reason. If the *McDonnell Douglas* framework is used, the proof structure might look like this: Higgins will have to prove a prima facie case: that he was a member of a protected class, that he was performing to expectations, that he experienced an adverse employment action, and that the employer continued to require the same amount and type of work to be done. This isn't exactly like the prima facie case in *McDonnell Douglas*, but the Court has made clear that the prima facie case is meant to be flexible and a sensible way to look at the evidence in the particular context of each case. The adverse employment action in *McDonnell Douglas* was a failure to hire, where here, the adverse employment action is a pay cut. These alterations seem to get at the same kinds of issues—requiring the plaintiff to disprove the main reasons they might experience a pay cut.

Higgins can prove a prima facie case. His protected class is his race, and there is no indication that anything about the quality of his work had changed. He seems to have been a good worker, getting progressively promoted to positions with greater responsibility over time. The adverse employment action has already been identified as a pay cut. Changes to compensation are explicitly identified in Title VII as potential unlawful employment actions if taken because of a person's protected class. Lastly, there is no indication that anything about the work of a line supervisor changed.

City Brewery will have to articulate a nondiscriminatory reason for the pay cut. The reason put forth by the new manager was that line supervisors were misclassified as hourly workers when they were really management. Note that given the description of the work done by line supervisors, I'm not sure that would be true for purposes of the Fair Labor Standards Act, but that is a different class, so I won't address a potential FLSA violation here. In any event, that reason is not itself race, so the employer will satisfy its burden with that. It also may say that this was a cost-cutting measure, and the fact that wage increases were denied to two shift managers who were white may support that.

Higgins will have the opportunity to demonstrate that this reason is just a pretext for discrimination. There are some facts that might be useful for that. First, the demographics of the position are relevant. Five of the 6 line supervisors are Black, and so even though this decision didn't only affect Black workers, the vast majority of workers affected were Black. Second, this *might* be an FLSA violation, which makes it seem like the employer was just looking for any excuse to pay these guys less, even a bad one. And third, the manager's comments have race-linked overtones, suggesting that perhaps he was thinking that Black employees should not make as much money as they were. Those comments, that most of the line supervisors would have been stuck cleaning the plant and that "we have come a long way" fairly clearly references a past where race discrimination kept Black employees in the lowest paid and dirtiest jobs in most workplaces. Additionally, the statement that the line supervisors "should be grateful" for their level of responsibility sounds like an intimation that because they were Black (because this was linked to past discriminatory working conditions), they didn't deserve the pay or positions they had.

Although a reasonable jury could conclude that race was the reason for the pay reduction, I worry that many factfinders would not conclude that. The comments are kind of subtle, and the presence of one white line supervisor might convince them that race was not the motive, but instead, the new manager was just making the bottleworks more financially stable, especially since wage increases for the two white shift managers were withheld. A factfinder might even conclude that race was a motivating factor, but that City Brewery would have made the same decision regardless because it made financial sense. If that is true, then even though City Brewery would be liable for discrimination, the remedies would be minimal.

### *Race Discrimination in Promotion*

The potential failure to promote case is a bit stronger. If Higgins uses the *McDonnell Douglas* framework, he will have to prove a prima facie case: that he was a member of a protected class, that he was qualified for and applied for the promotion, but the promotion was denied, and that the employer sought to fill the position with someone of Higgins's qualifications or did fill it.

Higgins can probably prove the prime facie case here, although there might be some challenges. He can prove that he was a member of a protected class, using his race, Black. And he applied for the promotion. Proving that he was qualified may be a little more challenging, because Simpson stated that to be considered for a shift manager position an applicant would need a college degree, which Higgins did not have. Additionally, he stated after the fact that he had also considered:

- experience in the brewing industry in a successful bottleworks
- leadership and organizational skills
- experience in more than one plant
- lack of association with main bottleworks

Higgins had some, but not all of these qualifications. Higgins had a good work history and had been promoted several times, which suggests that he had leadership and organizational skills, and he had experience in the brewing industry, although not outside the main bottleworks or at multiple plants. Still, he seems to have had the minimal qualifications for the promotion even without a college degree. Bolstering that, because it seems that the bottleworks promotes from within, and line supervisor is the position directly before shift manager, people who are line supervisors with enough experience are generally qualified to become shift managers. Higgins can, of course, show that he was denied the promotion. And he can prove that City Brewery filled those positions.

If Higgins successfully shows a prima facie case, City Brewery will articulate as its nondiscriminatory reason that the men who were promoted were more qualified. It is likely that City Brewery will especially highlight their experience outside of the main bottleworks.

Higgins then has an opportunity to show that this is a pretext for discrimination. He can do that by casting doubt on the employer's reason and/or providing additional evidence that points to race as the reason for the decision.

Because the qualifications issue in the prima facie case is a little challenging, Higgins might want to just simply use a comparator model of proof, comparing himself with the two people who were given the position. That model takes all of the evidence as a whole and considers whether a reasonable jury could conclude that race was the reason Higgins was denied the promotion. Alternatively, the additional evidence considered in this model could be considered evidence of pretext.

Higgins may want to take the asserted qualifications of the two men given the positions one at a time. First, he would want to highlight that they were both white, and that all 3 of the Black men who applied were denied the promotion. The only 2 white candidates (from the fact pattern) were given the position.

The employer's statements about the qualifications are suspect as well. Even though Simpson said that a college degree was required for the position, neither King nor Dade had a college degree. That Simpson stated this in the interview suggests he may even have been trying to discourage Higgins from applying.

And even though relevant experience in production seems to have been required, Dade did not have experience on the production line, based on the fact pattern. Instead, he was a maintenance supervisor, rather than having been a line supervisor. Additionally, his prior experience was at a bottleworks that was closed, not a successful one.

There are two additional things that cast doubt on the employer's asserted reasons. One is that it does not seem that either King or Dade actually applied for the position but were instead chosen for it. First, Higgins states that he does not recall a job posting or hearing about an application deadline. Second, King was working at another bottleworks when Simpson asked him to transfer. Additionally, Simpson seems to have provided different reasons for his decision to different people. He told the other two Black applicants that no internal person had applied in time.

Lastly, the full context of the working environment at City Brewery is relevant, as are Simpsons prior conduct and comments. Simpson spoke and ate lunch only with white employees, and he referred to Black employees as "boys." Referring to adult Black men as boys is a well known racial slight. All of this together could demonstrate that Simpson held race-based attitudes that influenced his decision-making process.

One last note. The strength of the failure to promote case may actually bolster the pay discrimination case and vice versa. If you look at each adverse action in isolation, it might be easier to find that financial reasons were behind the decision, but if you look at everything all together, there seems to be a bit more of a pattern reflecting that racial considerations pervaded the working environment and the decision-making process.

## Answer 4.

Ann, Brenda, and Cher clearly have a disparate impact sex discrimination claim, and they might even have a disparate treatment claim, although that would be weaker.

To state a claim for disparate impact discrimination, the plaintiffs will have to point to a specific employment practice that causes the disparity. Here, they would not point to the test *per se* but instead to the use of 90 as the functional cutoff score. The reason that they wouldn't use the test *per se* is that, at a passing score of 65, there is no disparate impact at all. Men and women score equally well at that level. The passing rate for women is 880/1200 x 100 = 73%, and the passing rate for men is 1320/1800 x 100 = 73%. The passing rates are identical.

It's only when the score used is 90 that there is a disparity on the basis of sex. There, the 90-score rate of women is 22/1200 x 100 = 2%, and for men is 198/1800 x 100 = 11%. Women passed at 18% the rate at which men passed (2/11 x 100 = 18%). This is well below the EEOC's 4/5ths (80%) threshold showing a presumptive disparate impact.

Thus, the employer will have to demonstrate that its use of the higher functional cutoff score is job related and consistent with business necessity. The employer will argue that the test used by the City to measure agility, endurance, strength and speed is strongly correlated to predict which applicants can successfully perform the strenuous physical tasks required of firefighters to protect public safety and save lives in emergency situations. Accordingly, it will argue, that score is job related and consistent with business necessity.

A cutoff score on an employment test that has discriminatory effects is permitted under Title VII as long as the employer can demonstrate that it "is job related and consistent with a business necessity." 42 U.S.C. § 2000e-2(k); *see also Griggs v. Duke Power Co.*, 401 U.S. 424 (1971); *Albemarle Paper Co. v. Moody*, 422 U.S. 405 (1975). A test's cutoff score will satisfy this requirement if it has been validated by an appropriate expert who has performed a job analysis and done a validation study. *Albemarle*; EEOC regulations. The fact pattern shows that the test was created and the cutoff score determined by an expert who first did a job analysis of the particular job in question. That expert also validated the test and score by professionally acceptable methods. After developing the employment test, the expert had the current Townsville firefighters take the test, the results of which she used to validate the predictive strength of the test. The expert then compared the results from the test to the number of commendations that each firefighter had received and found that firefighters who scored above a 90 on her test had the most commendations. This process of testing current firefighters and comparing their test scores with their commendation awards helped show that the employment test is a strong predictor of performing well. Thus, the analysis showed that the higher cutoff score is predictive of or significantly correlated with successful performance on the job as a whole. In other words, that correlation demonstrates the validity or predictive value of the higher cutoff score.

The plaintiffs might challenge a couple of things with both the creation of the test, and with the selection of the higher cutoff score. First, according to the City's job analysis, the job of firefighter requires a range of abilities, including physical abilities but also cognitive and social-emotional abilities. In fact, the ability most important to the job of firefighter is the ability to make decisions quickly when under pressure. The next most important ability is the ability to remain calm and follow directions when under pressure in an emergency. The third most important ability is the ability to work as part of a team to accomplish a task. Of the ten next most important abilities, only four are the physical abilities the performance test measures. The test the City used as a threshold screening device did not attempt to measure the abilities its own job analysis concluded are most important to performance as a firefighter.

The plaintiffs will then focus in on the use of 90 as the cutoff score. Ordinarily, a business necessity requires that a professionally developed test or credential be necessary as a *minimum qualification* for the job in question, appropriate to the entry level for that position. A cutoff score of 90 looks like a maximum qualification rather than a minimum qualification. And the City's own description of it is that it is aimed to produce people who could perform most tasks in only the most serious of emergencies. At the score of 65, on the other hand, nearly all of the applicants could accomplish all of the daily tasks of being a firefighter. It would seem that training could happen once firefighters are hired for the skills necessary for the most serious emergencies.

The City will respond with a couple of arguments. First, the test itself need not be defended, because it, by itself, does not appear to cause a disparate impact. Only when an employment practice causes a disparate impact will it have to be defended. Thus, the fact that only some skills were tested for is not a relevant consideration. Second, the plaintiffs' suggestion that the test must be tailored to particular skills is simply not how validity is measured. As long as the test measures some abilities essential to the job and accurately predicts job performance, the test will be valid. All that validity requires is a correlation between success on the test and success in the job. That correlation was demonstrated with the expert's validity test.

And responding to the argument about using 90 as the functional cutoff, the city may just push back on what that score represents. It might simply argue that as openings become available, it is considering everyone in the applicant pool, but choosing only among the most qualified. If the test is a valid predictor of success on the job, it seems that picking the highest scoring would simply comport with those results.

Additionally, even if a court were to find that the functional passing score was actually 90 rather than 65, it would likely defend that as a valid predictor. And it may use the context of this particular position and the needs of the department to show why in this situation 90 is actually a minimum qualification or at least close to one. It will likely draw on the 3rd Circuit's opinion in *Lanning v. SEPTA*, 181 F.3d 478 (3d Cir. 1999). There, the court considered a timed run as a test for transit police to satisfy the business necessity test even though transit police almost never had to run long distances quickly or do other tasks that required a particular aerobic capacity. In that case, the correlation between performance on that test and a high level of success on the job was enough, along with the fact that, in the court's view, women who trained more could pass the test. Although the court did not explicitly rely on the fact that the job was in the context of public safety, that fact still seemed very relevant. In public safety positions, greater physical fitness and strength capacity make an intuitive sense that courts may be unlikely to challenge.

The plaintiffs may then try to prove that alternative practices exist that would have less of a disparate impact on women but that would serve the needs of the employer equally well. The Fire Chief alluded to those alternative processes in the fact pattern. The challenge for the plaintiffs will be that the Fire Chief also suggested that those alternative practices were expensive to develop and use. The cost of those alternative practices may make them not truly available, and it is clear that they were not truly available at the time that this test was developed, because the city's resources were devoted to the development of this test.

Lastly, the plaintiffs might want to point to the duration of the city's knowledge of the disparate effects of the test along with some potentially stereotypical thinking about women and strength that might be motivating the city's decision makers to suggest that the use of this test is actually sex based disparate treatment. Usually, knowledge of a disparate impact is not enough to prove that the decision maker is motivated by the class of those disparately affected.

But over time, that knowledge and no effort to remedy the situation could eventually lead a factfinder to believe that the decision maker is retaining the test *because* of the impact that it has. In other words, over time, we might be more likely to believe that the city is retaining the test because it keeps women out of firefighting positions. And the Fire Chief's comments about women just having to work a little bit harder maybe in order to pass the test might suggest that he views women as less capable or less serious about firefighting. Those kinds of stereotypical views might also help to prove disparate treatment.

The disparate treatment case does not seem especially strong. It could be because public safety positions remain male dominated all across the country, and the stereotypes of women and men are still strongly influencing cultural notions about the job. There also do not seem to be individual instances of disparate treatment, which we might expect to see, or harassment, and the Fire Chief's comments are not especially sexist. All together, that seems to suggest something more subtle than what we expect disparate treatment to look like.

And the disparate impact challenge may not be successful, either. The City's business necessity defense is fairly strong, given the correlation between success on the test and success on the job. The one weak part is the use of that higher cutoff score, but even there, in a public safety context, a court may forgive a higher-than-minimum qualification.

# Additional Short Answer Questions

## Answer 1.

Employers can take a person's identity into account in at least four instances. First, an employer has to take employees' identities into account to guard against disparate impacts. Where employment practices impact one group significantly more than another, that practice will create an actionable disparate impact, so keeping track of the effects of employer practices requires considering employee identity characteristics.

Second, employers can take employees' identity into account when it is sex, national origin, religion, or age, and sex, national origin, religion or age is a bona fide occupational qualification for that particular job, necessary to the employer's business.

Third, employers have to take employees' religion or impairments/disability status into account in cases where employees seek accommodation for religious practices or to perform the essential functions of their job.

Fourth, employers can take employees' identity characteristics into account when there is a manifest imbalance in traditionally segregated job categories, and the employer acts pursuant to a valid affirmative action plan. An affirmative action plan will be valid when it is temporary, seeks to eradicate traditional patterns of segregation, and does not unnecessarily trammel the rights of non-beneficiaries.

There may be one more instance in which employers can consider an employee's identity characteristic, and that is where that consideration was not enough to make that identity a motivating factor, or even if it was, where the employer would have taken the same action without considering it. This last, where identity was a motivating factor but not a but-for cause, might not really count, since the employer will be liable—it just won't owe damages.

## Answer 2.

Mixed motives part 1: A mixed motives case is a case where both discriminatory and nondiscriminatory reasons motivated the employer's decision. A pretext case is where the discriminatory and nondiscriminatory reasons are offered as alternatives. So, in a mixed motives case, we acknowledge that a decision might have been made for multiple reasons. But in a pretext case, we are focused on a primary or predominant reason crowding other reasons out. Mixed motives are "yes, and" kinds of cases, while pretext cases are "either or" kinds of cases.

Mixed motives part 2: A plaintiff will want a mixed motives analysis when the evidence of discrimination is particularly weak. It might be in situations where a plaintiff can show a prima facie case and some reason to disbelieve the employer's reason but not necessarily a lot of great evidence that links the employer's decision to the plaintiff's protected class. In a mixed motives context, it will be easier for the plaintiff to get past summary judgment by saying that their protected class was merely a motivating factor rather than a but-for reason for the decision in that context. Conversely in a case where a plaintiff has an extremely strong case linking the employer's decision to their protected class, especially where there is direct evidence, an employer is going to want a mixed motives instruction. A mixed motives instruction gives the employer the opportunity to avoid the most serious remedies where it can demonstrate that the protected class was not a but-for reason for its decision—where it would have made the same decision without considering the plaintiff's protected class. In other words, a mixed motives instruction provides an employer something like a second bite at the apple to defend itself.

## Answer 3.

A. Yes, she should survive a motion to dismiss as long as she states that (1) the religious belief is sincerely held, (2) the employer had the chance to make an accommodation before Adams violated the dress code, and (3) Adams was penalized for conflicting with the dress code because of a religious practice based on her belief. She should likely survive a motion to dismiss because she should easily be able to satisfy these requirements. (i.e., her religious belief was sincerely held for three years and she had not worn pants since she converted; she informed Tasty Foods why she could not wear pants and they had the chance to offer an accommodation; and she was penalized by being fired).

B. I would want to explore what reasonable accommodation was offered, if any. If no reasonable accommodation was offered, then I would want to explore the reason behind the requirement of pants as a standard uniform. I would hope to find a reason that wearing a skirt would pose an undue hardship on the employer—maybe a safety concern, or hardship by entirely changing the dress code. However, I do not believe that an actual undue hardship will be found, so hopefully, the employer offered an accommodation.

## Answer 4.

A. The EEOC says that to be effective, an organization should have leadership committed and engaged to an environment free from discrimination, consistent and demonstrated accountability, strong and comprehensive harassment policies, trusted and accessible complaint procedures, and regular, interactive training tailored to the audience and the organization. An effective harassment policy should have a definition of the conduct prohibited in plain language, not overly legalistic, and examples of that conduct. It should be relatively short and readable. It should state clearly that it applies, at least, to all classes protected by law and that it applies to employees at all levels of the company. It should also explain how employees can file a complaint and provide multiple reporting channels. The policy should also state that the employer will provide a prompt, impartial, and thorough investigation and that the identity of those who report harassment will be kept confidential to the extent possible. There should also be a statement that retaliation will not be tolerated.

B. Tenderly should distribute its policy to all current employees and all new employees when they are hired. In addition to distributing the policy, the company leadership should meet and discuss the policy with employees and with supervisors and managers. Employees need to be able to recognize harassment and feel comfortable and confident knowing what to do when they see or experience it. Supervisors and managers should be trained separately on how to enforce this policy, educated on what their responsibilities are, and know what actions to take to prevent and remedy misconduct.

Once is also not enough. Employee meetings and trainings should be held at least on an annual basis not only to explain the policy but also to focus on tools like bystander interventions and civility in the workplace. Training that does not focus on the law may be more effective at changing the culture positively. In person training can be conducted in order to further enhance employees' understanding of what harassment looks like and the procedures to take when it is recognized. Finally, because it is very rare that employees who experience harassment will report it, Tenderly might think about an annual climate survey to assess whether harassment is happening but not being reported.

# Topical Index